ECOLOGY,
ECONOMY,
EQUITY

ALA Editions purchases fund advocacy,
awareness, and accreditation programs
for library professionals worldwide.

ECOLOGY, ECONOMY, EQUITY

The Path to a Carbon-Neutral Library

MANDY HENK

An imprint of the American Library Association

CHICAGO 2014

After her first day dusting copies of the Science Citation Index as a student assistant at Clark University (Worcester, Massachusetts) Science Library, **Mandy Henk** knew she had found her calling. A graduate of Simmons College School of Library Science and currently the Access Services Librarian at DePauw University in Greencastle, Indiana, Mandy devotes her time to activism, motherhood, writing, and librarianship. She was a 2011 Library Journal Mover and Shaker and one of the early guerrilla librarians of the People's Library at Occupy Wall Street. She rides an Xtracycle Radish and lives with her two children, husband, four cats, two frogs, and a dog.

© 2014 by the American Library Association

Printed in the United States of America

18 17 16 15 14   5 4 3 2 1

Extensive effort has gone into ensuring the reliability of the information in this book; however, the publisher makes no warranty, express or implied, with respect to the material contained herein.

ISBNs: 978-0-8389-1217-1 (paper); 978-0-8389-1968-2 (PDF); 978-0-8389-1969-9 (ePub); 978-0-8389-1970-5 (Kindle). For more information on digital formats, visit the ALA Store at alastore.ala.org and select eEditions.

Library of Congress Cataloging-in-Publication Data

Henk, Mandy.
    Ecology, economy, equity : the path to a carbon-neutral library / Mandy Henk. — First edition.
        pages   cm.
    Includes bibliographical references and index.
    ISBN 978-0-8389-1217-1 (alk. paper)
        1. Library buildings—Environmental aspects. 2. Library buildings—Energy conservation. 3. Libraries—Environmental aspects. 4. Libraries—Information technology. 5. Libraries and community. I. Title. II. Title: Path to a carbon-neutral library.
        Z679.85.H46 2014
        027—dc23   2014006000

Cover design by Kimberly Thornton. Images © Shutterstock, Inc.

Text composition by Dianne M. Rooney in the Chaparral, Gotham, and Bell Gothic typefaces.

♾ This paper meets the requirements of ANSI/NISO Z39.48-1992 (Permanence of Paper).

For Elliott and Hazel

and

In memory of Aaron Swartz

Contents

PART III
Sustainable Librarianship in Practice

Acknowledgments

Writing a book is a terribly difficult and time-consuming process. First, I owe thanks to Jamie Santos and Chris Rhodes at ALA Editions and their patience as the book-writing process dragged out far longer than I expected it to. Their support has been incredible.

I owe thanks to all of my colleagues at the DePauw Libraries, but especially to my director Rick Provine and my staff. Rick's willingness to give me the time I needed to write and my staff's incredible ability to keep the books flowing and doors open has been simply amazing. Candy Anderson, Connie Cree, Jamie Knapp, Jody Matthews, Meghan McCullough, Tina Oetken, Thea Warren, and Michelle Zimmerman will surely go down in history as the best, most skilled, and most dedicated library assistants in the history of libraries. Thanks also to Pheobe Migliano for her assistance in editing and fact-checking. I could not have finished this project without their support. Special thanks too to Bruce Sanders for reading every draft and providing valuable feedback. His thoughts and contributions have been invaluable to me, and I owe him a debt of gratitude. Thanks also to Meryl Altman and Kellie Dawson for reading early drafts and providing me the encouragement I needed to go on and to Jennifer Everett and Glen Kuecker for their encouragement and positive reaction when

I first asked if they thought a book on sustainability in libraries was a good idea.

Like many mothers, I struggle with finding an appropriate work-life balance. This book could not have been written without the many people who gave generously of their time to tend to my home and children while I worked. My husband, Chris Henk, whose willingness to take on more than his fair share of the household duties on occasion enabled me to write late at night and on weekends. Sara Crowe and her endless patience with my daughter and my somewhat unorthodox schedule. Ruth Poor and Taylor O'Brien who are the best combination nanny and research assistant any mother/author could ever want. Without them, I could not have written this book.

Finally, massive upsparkles to all my fellow guerrilla librarians at the People's Library at Occupy Wall Street. You have all provided me with inspiration, support, and the courage needed to write this book. You have been wonderful friends, great colleagues, and strong allies. Solidarity.

PART I

Transitioning to Sustainability in the Library

1
Librarianship and the Three Es

When I was a girl, there was a small creek that ran near my home. It wasn't really a creek, it was a drainage ditch designed to catch runoff from the houses around it and send the water into the sewage system. But its whole length was surrounded by trees and honeysuckle bushes, so it felt very much like a natural creek to me, especially since it usually had a small amount of water in it. Enough so that I and the other neighborhood children could pretend it was a creek and get good and muddy in it. When it rained hard, the ditch filled to the very brim and we could pretend it was a river. It never got too big to jump over though, and at the height of some summers it even dried up.

On May 3, 2010, I glanced at the news online from my office in Indiana and was startled to learn that my hometown of Nashville, Tennessee, was flooding. I watched in shock as pictures came over the web. Pictures of places I have known my whole life, now submerged under massive amounts of water. Places that I had never imagined flooding—nor had anyone else. The torrential rains only lasted for two days, but they brought almost 20 inches of rain and cost 31 lives. In Nashville, the amount of rain doubled the previous record for a two-day event. The Cumberland River crested at 51 feet, a level not seen since flood control measures were implemented in the 1960s. At the end of it, Nashville suffered an estimated $1.5 billion in damage. The symphony hall had sustained serious instrument loss, including two grand pianos and an organ. The Opry Mills mall, an important tourist destination, was destroyed by 10 feet of water—and did not reopen until 2012.[1]

The thing that really brought home the destruction, though, was the creek. The little drainage ditch that I had played in as child transformed into a raging river. It overran its concrete banks, knocked down honeysuckle bushes and young trees, and spilled out into the backyards and basements of families up and down the whole street. The little trickle of water, so small it dried up completely on occasion, had managed to bring mud and chaos to the bucolic street I called home for so many years.

For me, the flooding of Nashville brought home the need to take climate seriously and begin making changes in my life and in my work. For others, it may be the floods in Australia, Pakistan, Thailand, or Colombia;[2] it may be the droughts and wildfires in Colorado, Utah, Texas, Russia, France, and China;[3] it may be the anomalous tornado season of 2011[4] or the melting of the Arctic.[5] The thing about climate change is that it is global in scope and no one will escape its impact. In an interview with climate blogger Joe Romm, climatologist Kevin Trenberth, head of the Climate Analysis Section at the National Center for Atmospheric Research, said, "I find [the impact of global warming] systematically tends to get underplayed and it often gets underplayed by my fellow scientists. . . . it's unfortunate that the public is not associating these [weather events] with the fact that this is one manifestation of climate change. And the prospects are that these kinds of things will only get bigger and worse in the future."[6]

The scientific literature shows that the need to develop carbon neutral economies and societies has become even more urgent in recent years. The very best guidance produced by scientists is that we must reduce the carbon in our atmosphere to below 350 parts per million (ppm) and hold it there.[7] It might well need to be lower than that, but at the moment 350 ppm is the number believed to be the maximum amount of carbon in the atmosphere conducive to having a planet similar to the one onto which we were all born. Currently, our atmosphere is at 402 ppm and rising.[8] Even if we manage to accomplish the necessary reduction, a by no means certain accomplishment, it appears increasingly likely that some of the worst impacts predicted by the United Nation (UN) Intergovernmental Panel on Climate Change will not be prevented and must be mitigated against.[9]

What does all this mean to librarians? And what do we need to do to prepare our libraries for the world we have created—the world Bill McKibben has named Eaarth?[10] McKibben writes, "We've changed the planet, changed it in large and fundamental ways. And these changes are far, far more evident in the toughest parts of the globe, where climate change is already wrecking thousands of lives daily." He goes on to say, "We can't simply keep stacking boulders against the change that's coming on every front; we'll need to figure out what parts of our lives and our ideologies we must abandon so that we can protect the core of our societies and civilizations."[11] Climate change presents a very real threat to the world we have built and the world in which our libraries and the institutions they serve have thrived. The realities of climate change—both the already increased dangers we face and the urgent need to drastically reduce the amount of carbon we release into the atmosphere—require librarians to develop new practices in our collection building and programming as well as a new understanding of the natural world and our relationship to it. If we fail to make this transition, we risk being left behind in the scrap bin of history as a relic of the Carbon Age. If we succeed in this transition, we can help lead our communities and institutions forward into a new sustainable future, one with healthy libraries and a healthy ecosystem.

Sustainability, as an idea, grew out of the international development sphere. Development specialists understood that building economies that respected the natural environment was crucial if the populations supported by those economies were going to be self-supporting.[12] They also understood that a healthy economy is one that distributes its benefits throughout society. Because of this, sustainability is often thought of in terms of the three Es: ecology, equity, and the economy. Because human society and our interactions with the ecosystem are so complex, sustainability advocates argue that addressing challenges in these areas in a complementary fashion is necessary to prevent the solution to one problem from becoming a problem in another area. In other words, by considering both problems and solutions broadly, we can make decisions whose impacts are understood across multiple dimensions and reduce the possibly of unfortunate surprises down the road.

James Speth, the former dean of the Yale School of Forestry and Environmental Studies, in his book *The Bridge at the End of the World: Capitalism, the Environment, and Crossing from Crisis to Sustainability* identifies seven reactions that people commonly have to our current sustainability predicament:[13]

Resignation: All is lost.

Divine Providence: It's in God's hands.

Denial: What problem?

Paralysis: It's too overwhelming.

Muddling Through: It's going to be alright, somehow.

Deflection: It's not my problem.

Solutionist: Answers can and must be found.

Librarians need to take it upon ourselves to be Solutionists, both in our local communities and in our information system. We are living in a new and different world now than we were at the beginning of the information revolution, but mostly we haven't recognized the change yet. Libraries have a vitally important role going forward. To tackle the global threats we are facing as a society, we're going to need all the information literacy and lifelong learning we can muster and we're going to need it widely available. Librarians are responsible for protecting the public's right to information. If we are to enable our students, scholars, and citizens to counter the lies and propaganda about climate change coming from powerful and entrenched fossil fuel industries, we need to ensure their access to peer-reviewed science and authentic analysis, access that, as it stands now, lives far too often behind the expensive barrier of the corporate-owned and controlled scientific databases. We need to have citizens who are educated to carefully evaluate sources and who can distinguish between the emotional appeal of the propagandist and the objective data analysis of the scientist—a process that requires libraries staffed with well-trained librarians who have access to high-quality collections. In short, we need to create libraries of unparalleled excellence in both service and collections.

And yet, as enduring and as important as libraries should be, this is also a time when libraries are more vulnerable than ever to both external and internal shocks. Few libraries stand on their own; instead we are part of larger institutions—universities and colleges and cities and counties. As our home institutions thrive, we thrive, and when our home institutions suffer, so do we. Our budgets, our facilities, our staff, each of these is vulnerable to external shocks. The Great Recession that began in 2008 has been particularly harmful to library budgets. In 2009, *American Libraries Online* detailed tens of millions of dollars worth of budget cuts to academic libraries across the country.[14] In an Association of College & Research Libraries (ACRL) survey, librarians "overwhelmingly indicated" that "funding constraints, budget cutbacks, and declining support for and increasing costs of academic/research libraries are the most challenging issues" their libraries face.[15] Public libraries too are suffering from cutbacks. The state of California cut in half state funding for public libraries while also passing a trigger clause that could eliminate it completely.[16] Texas has eliminated its direct grant program to public libraries and also reduced funding for its state library programs by 88 percent.[17] My home state of Indiana has passed a constitutional property tax cap that all but ensures libraries will suffer serious cuts in the near future.[18]

But budget cuts are only one of the threats libraries are facing. We have also created an ecologically unsustainable dependence for ourselves and our users on a technological infrastructure that is gravely damaging to the environment. The servers and computers we and our users rely upon to deliver the content we have purchased are part of the carbon problem.[19] The combination of damage from energy use, mining of materials for electronic devices, and the damage caused from improper disposal of these devices is staggering. If we want to maintain the digital library that we have spent the last 20 years building, we need to find a way to transition to a technology that can be built and maintained without environmental destruction and without creating significant waste streams.

The technology we have grown so dependent on also rests upon a viciously exploitative labor system. And the abuses of this system are largely hidden from us and our users by a globalized production chain. Libraries are not unique in this respect—the globalization of production that took place in the past 30 years hid much labor abuse from consumers. The time to allow ourselves to overlook this abuse has passed. None of us would willingly purchase something we knew had been created under brutal management, but we have allowed ourselves the comfort of ignorance. When workers are literally killing themselves, dying from poison on the production line, and doing everything they can to improve their own lot, it behooves us to help them.[20] And that means using our power as institutional consumers to find alternatives.

The information revolution has another dark side as well—the consolidation of the publishing industry and the enclosure of the information commons. Both academic and general publishers have spent the past two decades engaged in a race to be the biggest company left standing.[21] The result of this race is a publishing industry dominated by large multinational corporations that are able to wield their considerable economic power for political gain. The book, magazine, and newspaper industry, dominated by Newscorp (owner of HarperCollins and FoxNews), McGraw-Hill, and Reed Elsevier spent almost $22 million in the last presidential election cycle. The industry spent an additional $12 million on lobbying in 2010.[22] These giants of the industry have one goal that unites them—protecting and extending copyright law and the continued erosion of fair use and the right of first sale. They wield their power not only in the halls of Congress, but also through the courts. The recent copyright case against Georgia State University for their e-reserves is an example of this abuse.[23] Outside of industry players, almost everyone agrees that the copyright law and fair use need to be updated to reflect technological changes and to respect the rights of the public, who in the case of academic publishing, are often the ones who funded the research anyway.[24]

Clearly, we have made a wrong turn. Overcoming the challenges we are facing requires us to look beyond practicality and to reexamine who we are and what we do as librarians. We are facing existential crises on multiple fronts: climate change and the immediate need to decarbonize our economy; the defunding and rapid "dismantling of the public sphere" and its attendant corporatization; the need to develop a technological infrastructure that is not based on the social and ecological exploitation that has been a core feature of globalization; and the enclosure of the information commons that has come silently with the information revolution.[25] Librarians are not unique in having to face multiple converging crises as we move through the 21st century, but we have been slow to recognize the building crisis. When we have advocated for change, we have been reformists and incrementalists, but the time for a slow agenda has passed. Earth's climate will not wait, and our obligation to the future is pressing. Just the like the information revolution rapidly swept through libraries, the sustainability revolution must sweep through faster than we think we can stand.

Transitioning to sustainability requires more than just measuring and reducing environmental impact. That tactic has been tried without success for many years. The time has come to try a new approach—recommitting to our fundamental values and reviewing our operations to ensure that they match those values. This is already well under way outside of the library. Paul Hawken has documented thousands and thousands of organizations building what he calls the "largest movement in the world."[26] Hawken describes this movement as "a collection of small pieces, loosely joined. It forms, dissipates, and then regathers quickly, without central leadership, command, or control."[27] He writes of the movement, "It will soon suffuse most institutions, but before then, it will change a sufficient number of people so as to begin the reversal of centuries of frenzied self-destructive behavior."[28] It is time to begin turning around the library we have built and aligning it with the future—with the movement to build a healthy and just world.

Reimagining the ethos and practice of librarianship to ensure that sustainability is brought to the forefront is a monumental task, and it is one that we need to undertake as a group, with voices from across the profession. Voices from small libraries and large, rich libraries and poor, and experienced librarians and newcomers to the profession, all have a stake in this conversation and all need to work together to guide the development of the future of librarianship. The task in front of us is nothing less than the matter of how we ensure that the accumulated knowledge of the world is preserved and made available to all the people of future generations, not only a small, privileged elite.

NOTES

1. "Epic Flood Event of May 2010," National Weather Service Weather Forecast Office, Nashville, TN, February 22, 2011, www.srh.noaa.gov/news/display _cmsstory.php?wfo=ohx&storyid=51780&source=0.; Michell, Lori and Heather Jensen, "Opry Mills Mall Reopens after 2 Years," WKRN, March 28, 2012, www.wkrn.com/story/17279361/opry-mills-mall-reopens-thursday.

2. David Fogarty, "Scientists See Climate Change Link to Australian Floods," *Reuters*, January 12, 2011, www.reuters.com/article/2011/01/12/

us-climate-australia-floods-idUSTRE70B1XF20110112; Nathaniel Gronewold, "Is the Flooding in Pakistan a Climate Change Disaster?" Climatewire, *Scientific American*, August 18, 2010, www.scientificamerican.com/article .cfm?id=is-the-flooding-in-pakist; "Climate Change Blamed for Thai Floods as UN Climate Talks Open," *Environment News Service*, April 6, 2011, www .ens-newswire.com/ens/apr2011/2011-04-06-02.html; Autumn Spanne, "Colombia's Cities Risk Deluge from Changes in Andes Climate," *The Daily Climate*, December 3, 2012, www.dailyclimate.org/tdc-newsroom/2012/12/ colombia-andes-flooding.

3. Michael Finneran, "Wildfires: A Symptom of Climate Change," NASA, September 24, 2010, www.nasa.gov/topics/earth/features/wildfires.html.

4. Martin Hoerling, "Preliminary Assessment of Climate Factors Contributing to the Extreme 2011 Tornadoes" (draft research assessment), Physical Sciences Division, Earth System Research Laboratory, National Oceanic and Atmospheric Administration, updated July 8, 2011).

5. "Global Warming Puts the Arctic on Thin Ice," Natural Resources Defense Council, last modified November 22, 2005, www.nrdc.org/globalwarming/ qthinice.asp.

6. Joe Romm, "Exclusive Interview: NCAR's Trenberth on the Link between Global Warming and Extreme Deluges," *Climate Progress*, accessed October 22, 2013, http://thinkprogress.org/climate/2010/06/14/206133/ ncar-trenberth-global-warming-extreme-weather-rain-deluge.

7. James Hansen et al., "Target Atmospheric CO_2: Where Should Humanity Aim?" *Open Atmospheric Science Journal* 2, no. 1 (2008): 217–31.

8. "Trends in Carbon Dioxide," Global Monitoring Division, Earth System Research Laboratory, National Oceanic and Atmospheric Administration, May 6, 2013, www.esrl.noaa.gov/gmd/ccgg/trends.

9. A. P. Sokolov et al., "Probabilistic Forecast for Twenty-First-Century Climate Based on Uncertainties in Emissions (without Policy) and Climate Parameters," *Journal of Climate* 22, no. 19 (2009): 5175–204; Laura E. Coristine and Jeremy T. Kerr, "Habitat Loss, Climate Change, and Emerging Conservation Challenges in Canada," *Canadian Journal of Zoology* 89, no. 5 (2011): 435–51.

10. Bill McKibben, *Eaarth: Making a Life on a Tough New Planet*, (New York: Times Books, 2010).

11. Ibid., xiii.

12. "Our Common Future," United Nations, World Commission on Environment and Development (1987).

13. James Gustave Speth, *The Bridge at the End of the World: Capitalism, the Environment, and Crossing from Crisis to Sustainability* (New Haven, CT: Yale University Press, 2008), 42.

14. Leonard Kniffel, "Cuts, Freezes Widespread in Academic Libraries," *American Libraries* 40, no. 67 (2009): 28.

15. Ibid.

16. Michael Kelley, "In California, All State Funding for Public Libraries Remains in Jeopardy," *Library Journal* (July 5, 2011), http://lj.libraryjournal.com/2011/07/budgets-funding/in-california-all-state-funding-for-public-libraries-remains-in-jeopardy.

17. Michael Kelley, "Texas Governor Signs Budget Cutting State Funding for Library Services by 88%," *Library Journal* (July 29, 2011), http://lj.library journal.com/2011/07/budgets-funding/texas-governor-signs-budget-cutting-state-funding-for-library-services-by-88-percent/#_.

18. Maureen Hayden, "Opponents of Amendment to Put Tax Caps in Constitution Face Uphill Battle," *Herald Bulletin*, October 6, 2010.

19. David L. Gard and Gregory A. Keoleian, "Digital Versus Print: Energy Performance in the Selection and Use of Scholarly Journals," *Journal of Industrial Ecology* 6, no. 2 (2003): 115–32.

20. "iPhone Workers Say 'Meaningless' Life Sparks Suicides," *Bloomberg News*, June 2, 2010, www.bloomberg.com/news/2010-06-02/foxconn-workers-in-china-say-meaningless-life-monotony-spark-suicides.html; Jeffrey Kaye, "In China, Factory Workers Allege Poisoning from iPhone Production," *PBS NewsHour* video, 7:25, April 13, 2011, www.pbs.org/newshour/bb/world/jan-june11/china_04-13.html; David Barboza and Keith Bradsher, "In China, a Labor Movement Aided by Modern Technology," *New York Times*, June 16, 2010.

21. "Hot Topics: Publisher Mergers," UC Berkeley Libraries, November 8, 2011, www.lib.berkeley.edu/scholarlycommunication/publisher_mergers.html.

22. "Books, Magazines, and Newspaper Industries," Center for Responsive Politics, www.opensecrets.org. accessed April 26, 2014.

23. Andrew Richard Albanese, "A Failure to Communicate," *Publishers Weekly*, June 4, 2010, www.publishersweekly.com/pw/by-topic/industry-news/publisher-news/article/43500-a-failure-to-communicate.html.

24. For example, see Siva Vaidhyanathan, *The Anarchist in the Library: How the Clash between Freedom and Control Is Hacking the Real World and Crashing the System* (New York: Basic Books, 2004).

25. John Buschmann, *Dismantling the Public Sphere: Situating and Sustaining Librarianship in the Age of the New Public Philosophy* (Westport, CN: Libraries Unlimited, 2003).

26. Paul Hawken, *Blessed Unrest: How the Largest Movement in the World Came into Being, and Why No One Saw It Coming* (New York: Viking, 2007).

27. Ibid., 12.

28. Ibid., 189.

2

The Case for Sustainability in the Library

Sustainability is a trendy idea—one bragged about by corporations, argued over by philosophers, and often given lip service by those in power. But what is it? And what does it mean to create a sustainable society and a sustainable library? How can we reconceptualize our existing values so that sustainability can take precedence while still honoring our profession's legacy and values? What kinds of changes do we need to make to create the kind of library and information ecosystem that sustainability demands—one based on the principles of ecological, social, and economic justice?

LIBRARY VALUES

Before we can consider the question of how to apply the precepts of sustainability to librarianship, it is worth taking a close look at who we are as a profession. What values do we hold dear, and what values define our relationship to ourselves and to our communities and vendors? The information revolution of the past few decades has deeply shaken the profession and altered the landscape in profound ways. Combine that change with a period in American history that has been defined by the rise of market fundamentalism and the steep decline of the public sector, and it is no wonder that librarians are struggling to define ourselves and our missions. Competing camps argue for a transition to a fully digital library, for a new role as "conversion facilitators," for a renewed focus on our role as technologists and promoters of the techno-future.[1] The profession can come across as defensive and contradictory, even confused. Despite the differences though, there are many commonalties between the competing visions of librarianship—commonalities that are based in a widely shared vision of the profession and its role in society. This common vision and the values that underlie it point our way forward, toward a more sustainable library.

Not long ago, I was in a meeting with two salespeople, young and earnest, they were representing a large publisher who was trying to sell my library an extensive e-book collection. We asked all of the usual questions about the scope of the collection, Digital Rights Management issues, what formats would be available to our patrons and so on. At the end of the meeting, I asked, as gently as possible, what the carbon footprint of the servers would be. Flummoxed, the poor saleswoman sputtered and asked, quite seriously, "Is this a normal question?" Immediately following the meeting , one of the salespeople, a very young man fresh out of college, said to me, "I was an environmental studies major in college. I don't know why I never thought about the impact of our servers before." He promised to investigate and follow up as soon as he could. A year later, I received a rather sheepish response providing general information about the impact of large server operations. His employer was not able to provide any specific information nor was it inclined to share even basic information that would allow me to investigate on my own.

Values tell us what questions to ask, but they also require a certain kind of discipline to maintain, especially in the face of complex issues that constantly require us to weigh one value against another. Fortunately for us, library values and sustainability fit quite well together, making the transition we are facing far less challenging than it could be otherwise. Broadly speaking, library values can be sorted into three categories, each representing an important aspect of our profession.[2] The first, and most important, is the value of democracy. Whether arguing for a more technological, a more traditional, or a new kind of library altogether, virtually all librarians agree, at least in their rhetoric, that libraries exist because our society believes in self-governance and that our profession plays an important role in providing access to information for citizens. Second is the value of scholarship. Across the profession and going back to its earliest days, the value of rational objective scholarship in the service of education and society is affirmed. Respect for scholarship drives the way we organize information and how we help people to use that information.

Third, stewardship, the idea that we act not as owners or creators, but rather as careful maintainers and organizers of society's records, ideas, and stories is fundamental to who we are and what we do. Our role as information stewards is an important, and exclusive to our profession, long-term contribution to the present and to the next generation.

From the value of democracy flow other values. Equality, both of opportunity and circumstance. Intellectual freedom, which is understood by our profession as a necessary component of political freedom. Universal literacy, so that everyone can understand current issues and debates and has the tools needed to participate. All of these ideals are fundamentally based on the idea that a free and self-governing people require the free and open flow of information as well as the means to use and understand that knowledge in order to flourish. Each of these values animates our profession and drives our decision making. Because we care about equality, we design services and buildings that are open and welcoming to as many people as possible. Because we care about intellectual freedom, we fight for our patrons' privacy and ensure that we offer balanced collections that provide access to a wide range of ideas and points of view. Because universal literacy is important to us, we spend considerable amounts of money and time designing and implementing programming and building collections to support both children and adult learners. Democracy, and our role in protecting democracy, drives our sense of who we are as a profession and gives meaning to what might otherwise be frustrating and often challenging work.

Scholarship, as a library value, is rooted in our role as purveyors of knowledge. As librarians, we, and the buildings and collections we create, embody a commitment to education and to the value of the human narrative we so carefully gather and preserve. The debate over what to add to our collections, what to preserve, and how to balance our role as educators with our desire to remain relevant in an age when the deluge of information is overwhelming is a reflection of the role that scholarship has traditionally played in the profession. From the value we place on scholarship we also derive the values of reason and impartiality. Reason, the idea that informed inquiry and rational thought can be used to increase our understanding of the world, is an important part of why libraries exist. What use are all of our books and resources if the knowledge they can impart cannot enhance our understanding and help us solve the challenges we face? Impartiality is also an important value that derives from our commitment to scholarship. We offer all points of view on our shelves and in our collections and allow the ideas within them to stand, or fall, on their own. We are not, however, completely neutral. When working with patrons and allocating scarce dollars, we privilege the original, the well-written, the accurate over the repetitive, the impenetrable, and the just plain wrong. These designations are often controversial and lead to debate both within the profession and within our communities, but they also tend to reaffirm our commitment to the value of scholarship and reading as a method of inquiry and learning.

Stewardship as a library value has two important aspects. The first is the preservation of content itself. The rise of digital formats has placed considerable strain on our ability to live up to this value, but most of us still make strong attempts to preserve for future readers what we can and to build collections that will continue to have value in the future and to the future. When we develop digital repositories and dark archives, we are acting on the value of stewardship. When we proceed with caution as new formats arise and replace old formats, we are being wise and careful stewards of our collection. The second aspect of stewardship within the profession has evolved in the face of the assault on the legal basis of our profession—the preservation of the legal rights of the public to both access and use the knowledge that we have gathered. We are living the value of stewardship when we advocate within the public sphere for the protection of the right of first sale, for fair use, and for limits on the rights of copyright owners to replace public law with the private law of contracts through licensing rather than purchase. When we negotiate with vendors for perpetual access to a resource instead of temporary, annually billed access, we are using the value of stewardship to spend wisely and build permanent collections that will serve long into the future, even in times of budgetary crisis.

Libraries have an almost unique place in American society in the early 21st century; they serve as one of the few remaining functioning commons in an era dominated by enclosed spaces and resources. Understanding the idea of the common and the role it plays in building a healthy society is crucially important because many current sustainability problems are directly related to a failure to manage the common in a healthy and just way. The famous essay by Garrett Hardin, "The Tragedy of the Commons," is often cited as an example of why enclosing commons is a positive development.[3] Considerable criticism since that essay was published has refuted his claims that commons were destined to failure.[4] The primary error Hardin made was failing to recognize that all commons are not free-for-alls where anyone is entitled to claim all they wish. In actual practice, commons can be carefully managed resources whose benefits and privileges are clearly delineated through both written documents and social custom. Because librarians have considerable experience managing commons, it is after all the bulk of our daily work, we are in a good position to apply that knowledge to the sustainability crises and begin developing newer, saner, paths forward.

SUSTAINABILITY

Sustainability is built on the idea of intra- and intergenerational justice—the notion that those currently living have an obligation to themselves and to future people to ensure everyone has equal opportunities in life. Despite the simplicity of its basic precepts, sustainability is a complex idea, one whose history and development over the years have refined it from an awkward compromise between competing factions into a powerful and influential ideology. The concept itself rests on an analysis of human society, specifically industrialized society, which is both moral and empirical. On the moral side are those who argue that we have an obligation to future generations to leave them a planet that is not only habitable, but also allows them the same opportunities to pursue a good life that we currently enjoy. On the empirical side are scientists, including climate researchers, ecologists, and biologists, presenting data that demonstrate that the physical systems of the planet and the biosphere are showing signs of serious degradation due to human activities. They argue that the continuation of common practices like burning fossil fuels, cutting down forests, and intensive monocrop agriculture are creating risks, both for the present generation and for generations to come.

HISTORY OF THE IDEA

One of the earliest mentions of "sustainable" as a worthy social goal was by the World Council of Churches in 1974.[5] Introduced in a report on the use of science and technology for human development, the idea of a "sustainable society" was defined both in ecological terms, "a robust global society will not be possible unless the need for food is at any time well below the global capacity to supply it and unless the emissions of pollutants are well below the capacity of the ecosystems to absorb them," and in terms of equity, "social stability cannot be obtained without an equitable distribution of what is in scarce supply or without common opportunity to participate in social decisions."[6] This idea, sustainability as a value that required both equality within society and care for the ecosystem, would be echoed in the influential Brundtland Report 13 years later.

The release of the Brundtland Report is considered by many the genesis of the sustainability movement.[7] Titled "Our Common Future," it was published by the UN World Commission on Environment and Development (WCED) in 1987 and serves as the primary foundational document of the sustainability movement to this day. The WCED was set up by the UN General Assembly to "propose long-term environmental strategies for achieving sustainable development to the year 2000 and beyond." At the time, the conflict between development specialists and environmentalists over how to best serve the nations of the global South was intense.[8] The commission was to find a way to resolve this conflict so that development could continue along a new path, one that was both ecologically and socially sound.

The Brundtland Report defined sustainable development as "development which meets the needs of the present without compromising the ability of future generations to meet their own needs."[9] Like the World Council of Churches before it, the WCED focused on the role of eliminating poverty and global inequities in resource use: "Poverty is not only an evil in itself, but sustainable development requires meeting the basic needs of all and extending to all the opportunity to fulfill their aspirations for a better life. A world in which poverty is endemic will always be prone to ecological and other catastrophes." The report continued, "Meeting essential needs requires not only a new era of economic growth for nations in which the majority are poor, but an assurance that those poor get their fair share of the resources required to sustain that growth."[10] Beyond that, the report also recognized the increasing risks posed by new technologies: "The future—even a sustainable future—will be marked by increasing risk. The risks associated with new technologies are growing. The numbers, scale, frequency, and impact of natural and human-caused disasters are mounting."[11] This basic challenge, poverty and the need for economic growth, balanced against the risks of new technologies and increased industrialization, stands as the conflict that sustainability aims to resolve.

PHILOSOPHICAL INTERPRETATIONS AND DEBATES

Sustainability is sometimes talked about as a "contestable concept" which is a way of acknowledging that it can mean different things in different contexts and from within different ideological perspectives.[12] Michael Jacobs argues that sustainability is similar in this way to ideas like justice or democracy. Like justice or democracy, sustainability can be understood as a two-layered concept. The first layer is easily agreed to and widely supported. After all, everyone in our profession supports democracy and justice. And indeed, who would argue that we should engage in unsustainable behavior or develop unsustainable systems? It is in the second layer of meaning, Jacobs argues, "where the contest occurs: political argument over how the concept should be interpreted in practice." The idea itself and its adoption as a "normative goal" is fully accepted by virtually everyone; it is only in the second level, the applied level, that real political struggle and debate take place.[13]

Sustainability is also generally understood as coming in two forms, strong and weak.[14] Weak sustainability accepts the idea of substitutability. In other words, proponents of weak sustainability argue that, when considering intergenerational justice, what really matters is the overall package that we hand down. So that while we may hand down a degraded environment, we can balance that by ensuring that the human capital we pass on is sufficient to make up the difference. Proponents of strong sustainability do not accept the idea that human capital can substitute for environmental benefits. They argue that some environmental services, most especially life-support services, do not have a human substitute. They also argue that, on a human timescale at least, environmental goods and services are irreplaceable once destroyed. So if we handed down a degraded environment, but future generations decided that they wanted an intact environment, there would be no way for those future people to restore the damage. Finally, they argue that the Earth system is highly complex and that it is impossible to know the exact impacts of environmental degradation until after the fact and so it is best to limit impacts rather than risk an unforeseen catastrophe.

The nature of sustainability as a broad concept with many different interpretations leaves it vulnerable to charges of weakness. However, Jacobs and others argue that these charges are baseless.[15] Their arguments are twofold. First, sustainability does have a consistent set of values across the discourse, including the integration of the environment and the economy, a concern for environmental protection, a focus on both intra- and intergenerational equity, a claim that quality of life and income are not interchangeable, and a commitment to participatory forms of decision making and government. Second, despite strong opposition from powerful interests, sustainability has been strongly influential across many different areas of human activity. Governments, corporations, universities all want to be seen as sustainable and support sustainability in word if not deed.

ECOLOGICAL ECONOMICS

While the concept of sustainability originated in the international development sphere, it has also been taken up by economists who seek to apply its principles to the economic systems that sustain our material needs and wants. The field of ecological economics, which is distinct from environmental economics, frames its understanding of the economy as a subsystem of the larger planetary system and takes the sustainability of economic activity as one of its primary aims. Ecological economists argue that, because the economy is thoroughly dependent on the biophysical systems of the planet for raw materials, life-support services, and pollution sinks (the ability of the planet to absorb waste and pollution), the economy must be structured to respect the physical behavior of the Earth. In their view, the correct scale is one that allows renewable resources to renew themselves, wastes to be absorbed with limited damage to the environment, and nonrenewable resources to be recycled as much as possible.[16] Herman Daly, the author of the 1978 book that introduced the idea of a steady state economy, *Steady-State Economics*, describes it this way: "The economy is a wholly owned subsidiary of the environment, not the reverse."

SCIENTIFIC SUPPORT

The moral and ethical arguments for sustainability are themselves persuasive, but in order to begin implementing sustainable practices and to fully understand what a sustainable industrialized world would look like, it is important to understand the scientific evidence regarding environmental destruction and the stability of the Earth system. One of the most common arguments against the transition to sustainability is that the Earth is in fact quite healthy and capable of supporting an even larger and more affluent population.[17] Unfortunately, even an overview of the state of the Earth's biosphere, resource base, and pollution sinks reveals that we are pushing against the limits of the Earth's ability to support us. Concerns about the impact of economic and population growth sit at the center of the scientific argument for sustainability and date back to the earliest days of the movement. In fact, one of the founding scientific documents of the sustainability movement is titled *Limits to Growth*.[18] The 1972 study was authored by a group of Massachusetts Institute of Technology (MIT) researchers and was first published by the Club of Rome. It was the first attempt to use computer modeling to explore the relationships of growth in population, resource use, and industrial output to the finite resources available to us. *Limits to Growth* helped define the terms of the public debate and brought the question of unlimited growth on a finite planet into stark relief. It is also worth noting that, 30 years after the publication of the book, outside researchers have demonstrated that the world is indeed following the projections of the computer model, known as the "business as usual" scenario, that leads to catastrophic population collapse in the middle of the 21st century.[19]

The basic problem the *Limits to Growth* study illuminated is that of exponential growth. Humans have developed many clever riddles to help each other understand exponential growth; my favorite is the one about the child and the allowance. In that riddle a child is arguing with her parents for a larger allowance. The parents refuse, but the child makes a counteroffer: she'll take a lower allowance, down to one penny a week even, as long as it doubles each week for a year. The parents, outsmarted by their child, agree. After one year, how large is the child's allowance? Twenty-two and half trillion dollars. Per week. Lester Brown of the Earth Policy Institute used another well-known riddle as the title of one of his books on sustainability, *The Twenty-Ninth Day*.[20] That riddle begins on a pond with a few lily pads dotting the surface of the water. Each day the lily pads double in number. If the pond is fully covered by lily pads on the thirtieth day, how many days will it take until the pond is half covered? Twenty-nine days. The lily pad story highlights how things that seemed small and manageable suddenly grow large and out of control when growing exponentially. On the twenty-ninth day everything is fine on the pond. There is ample room for fish and birds. Nothing seems to be amiss, yet the very next day the pond is choked by the lily pads. The real-world implications of exponential growth can be dramatic.

Exponential growth in the human population and industrial activity has clearly had many different negative impacts. Whether you consider the ongoing loss of songbirds across the United States, the decline in the numbers of monarch butterflies in the Midwest and Mexico, or the threat to the spotted owl in the Pacific Northwest, biodiversity and species loss certainly stands out as one of the most charismatic environmental catastrophes we are facing. And a catastrophe it is. The UN Millennium Ecosystem Assessment, published in 2005, found, "Between 10% and 50% of well-studied higher taxonomic groups (mammals, birds, amphibians, conifers, and cycads) are currently threatened with extinction."[21] To put it another way, within as little as 300 years at the current rate, we will have lost enough species to have had a mass extinction event of the magnitude of those that occurred at the end of the Ordovician, Devonian, Permian, Triassic, and Cretaceous periods.[22] According to the UN's Convention on Biological Diversity, held in 2010, the causes of this enormous loss are solely human created: habitat loss and degradation, climate change, excessive nutrient load and other forms of pollution, over-exploitation and unsustainable use, and invasive alien species.[23]

While the loss of a few birds and butterflies is certainly sad, the consequences of the loss go much deeper. A reasonably objective and easily quantifiable way of understanding the value of biodiversity is through the concept of ecosystem services. Different researchers have categorized ecosystem services in a variety of taxonomies, but the one offered by the Millennium Ecosystem Assessment is the most straightforward: provisioning services, regulating services, cultural services, and supporting services.[24] Provisioning services include those goods that come directly from nature and are themselves immediately useful to people, things like trees and fish. Regulating services are those interactions that maintain a livable climate, atmosphere, and other vital services. Cultural services include the aesthetic and spiritual value that people attach to nature. Finally, supporting services are processes like soil formation that do not immediately benefit humans but are nonetheless vital to maintaining a livable planet.[25] Various research groups have valued these services at between $16 and $54 trillion.[26] Given the value of the services provided by the ecosystem, it seems only sensible to do all we can to protect its health. Without a healthy ecosystem, the smooth functioning and resilience of the systems that we are adapted to, the systems whose smooth functioning make our planet habitable, are at risk.[27]

While the services that come directly from the ecosystem are crucially important, human society, especially industrialized society, also relies heavily on nonliving resources to support itself. Energy and fresh water are especially crucial. They are also both under considerable pressure from overexploitation. Energy in particular is beginning to strain our national economy and the economies of other Western nations. In the United States we consume more than 18 million barrels of petroleum products per day, 2.74 million short tons of coal per day, and nearly 70 billion cubic feet of natural gas per day.[28] This is supplemented by an additional 266 trillion BTUs of energy derived from renewable sources including water, wind, and solar.[29] The problem of tightening energy supplies is not limited to the United States. Since 2005, overall worldwide oil production has been on an undulating plateau. During that time, the global prices of oil, coal, and other fossil fuel resources have doubled and become even more unstable.[30] These price increases have allowed new forms of extraction, especially tar sands mining and hydraulic fracturing, to become profitable. While these nonconventional sources do help alleviate the supply issues, there is ample evidence that these are even more profoundly dangerous and damaging to both humans and the natural environment than conventional fossil fuels.[31]

Fresh water is also becoming increasingly scarce. Just within the United States, where 140 million people rely on groundwater to meet their needs, there is widespread depletion of aquifers ranging from the north Atlantic region to Florida, across the Great Plains, and all the way to California.[32] Rivers too are facing pressure from both overuse and changing weather patterns. The Colorado River, the main water source for central California's fruit and vegetable growing region, is at risk of being unable to provide the needed water on a regular basis as early as 2025.[33] Even more worrying is the global situation. The glaciers that supply water to both the Yangtze and the Ganges rivers are rapidly melting.[34] The fossil aquifer that allowed Saudi Arabia to be self-sufficient in wheat production is already so depleted that Saudi Arabia has stopped wheat subsidies and expects to rely entirely on imports as early as 2016.[35] Other water hot spots include Yemen, the countries of North Africa, and central China. As these glaciers and aquifers deplete, the populations that rely on them for agriculture will be forced to seek out food on world grain markets. As the demand for grain increases from increasing population, increased affluence, and a reduction in arable land, the price of food will rise rapidly. Throw in a further reduction in land available to grow food, due to the conversion of cropland to biofuel production, and the stage is set for a real crisis.

Many analysts believe that this combination was in part responsible for the food price spikes of 2008 and 2011.[36]

While the Earth provides us with the biological and nonbiological resources we need to sustain our global civilization, it also serves as a pollution sink—absorbing our wastes and recycling them. In this too, there is ample evidence that we are at the end of the planet's ability to meet our current demands. The prime example of this is, of course, climate change and its sister problem, ocean acidification. In the years since the last full Intergovernmental Panel on Climate Change (IPCC) report in 2007, there has been considerable research demonstrating that the situation is even more dire than was understood at the time. The relative safety of limiting the global average surface temperature to the 2°C level, previously thought to represent a level where "dangerous anthropogenic impacts" would be limited, has been called into question.[37] Data now show that 2°C of warming above the preindustrial level presents far more risk than was previously understood.[38] At the same time, the previous hope of limiting global warming to 2°C is now dimming. Researchers at MIT, using advanced modeling techniques, have found that without quick action there is a 90 percent probability of a rise in global temperatures in the 3.5°C–7.4°C range, with a median projected warming of 5.1°C, by 2100.[39] Other researchers have found similar ranges to be likely given the current reluctance by governments to begin seriously limiting carbon emissions.[40]

What does a world with 5.1°C of warming look like? The 4 Degrees and Beyond International Climate Conference explored this question. Researchers looked at various impacts across agriculture, forest health, sea-level rise, natural disasters like flooding and drought and painted a bleak picture indeed. A themed issue of *Philosophical Transactions of the Royal Society A: Mathematical, Physical, and Engineering Sciences* based on the conference covered the impacts in detail.[41] Massive population migration due to climate impacts, catastrophic sea-level rise leading to the displacement of up to 187 million people, increased drought in already water-stressed regions, including within the United States, and extreme regional temperature increases (6°C) are all likely impacts in a 4°C+ world.

THE SUSTAINABILITY MOVEMENT

The good news is that we are now reaching a tipping point of sorts. The idea of sustainability and recreating our world to build healthy, resilient communities is spreading and blossoming into a full-fledged social movement. Social movements are incredibly powerful forces for change. They can make what might now seem impossible and futile become inevitable. And the social movement for sustainability is rapidly building critical mass. Since Paul Hawken published his book on the movement, *Blessed Unrest*, in 2007 the movement has virtually exploded.[42] Even the *Harvard Business Review* has identified sustainability as the next big megatrend.[43] From the Transition Town movement to the Occupy movement, sustainability is a flourishing idea—one that stands ready to find a new path forward, one based on care for the resources that sustain us and for each other.

NOTES

1. For examples, see Marianne Ryan and Julie Garrison, "What Do We Do Now?: A Case for Abandoning Yesterday and Making the Future," *Reference & User Services Quarterly* 51, no. 1 (Fall 2011): 12–14; R. David Lankes, *The Atlas of New Librarianship* (Cambridge, MA: MIT Press, 2011), http://mitpress-ebooks.mit.edu/product/atlas-new-librarianship.

2. I am indebted to Michael Gorman for his work on library values. Michael Gorman, *Our Enduring Values: Librarianship in the 21st Century* (Chicago: American Library Association, 2000).

3. Garrett Hardin, "The Tragedy of the Commons," *Science* 162, no. 3859 (1968): 1243–48.

4. Elinor Ostrom, *Governing the Commons: The Evolution of Institutions for Collective Action* (New York: Cambridge University Press, 1990).

5. Simon Dresner, *The Principles of Sustainability*, 2nd ed. (London: Earthscan, 2008), 1.

6. Ibid., 32.

7. "Our Common Future," United Nations, World Commission on Environment and Development (1987).

8. Ibid., Chairman's Foreword.

9. Ibid., Section 3.27.

10. Ibid., Section 3.27.

11. Ibid., Section 3.56.

12. Michael Jacobs, "Sustainable Development as a Contested Concept," in *Fairness and Futurity: Essays on Environmental Sustainability and Social Justice*, ed. Andrew Dobson (New York: Oxford University Press, 1999).

13. Ibid., 25.

14. Konrad Ott, "The Case for Strong Sustainability," in *Greifswald's Environmental Ethics: From the Work of the Michael Otto Professorship at Ernst Moritz Arndt University 1997–2002*, ed. Konrad Ott and Philipp Pratap Thapa (Greifswald, Germany: Steinbecker, 2003).

15. Michael Jacobs, "Sustainable Development as a Contested Concept," 26–30.

16. Herman E. Daly, *Ecological Economics and Sustainable Development: Selected Essays of Herman Daly* (Cheltenham, UK: Edward Elgar, 2007).

17. For the classic example of this argument, see Julian Lincoln Simon, *The Ultimate Resource* (Princeton, NJ: Princeton University Press, 1981).

18. Donella H. Meadows, *The Limits to Growth; A Report for the Club of Rome's Project on the Predicament of Mankind* (New York: Universe Books, 1972).

19. Graham Turner, "A Comparison of the Limits to Growth with Thirty Years of Reality," CSIRO Working Paper 2008-09, Socio-Economics and the Environment in Discussion, Commonwealth Scientific and Industrial Research Organisation, Australia, June 2008; Charles A. S. Hall and John W. Day Jr., "Revisiting the Limits to Growth after Peak Oil," *American Scientist* 97, no. 3 (2009).

20. Lester R. Brown, *The Twenty-Ninth Day: Accommodating Human Needs and Numbers to the Earth's Resources* (New York: Norton, 1978).

21. Tundi Agardy et al., *Ecosystems and Human Well-Being: Biodiversity Synthesis* (Washington, DC: World Resources Institute, 2005), 5.

22. Anthony D. Barnosky, "Has the Earth's Sixth Mass Extinction Already Arrived?" *Nature* 471, no. 7336 (2011).

23. Convention on Biological Diversity, Ecosystem Services (Montreal, Quebec: Secretariat of the Convention on Biological Diversity, 2010).

24. Agardy et al., *Ecosystems and Human Well-Being: Biodiversity Synthesis*, 19.

25. For more detailed definitions, see Diversity, "Ecosystem Services."

26. Robert Costanza et al., "The Value of the World's Ecosystem Services and Natural Capital," *Nature* 387, no. 6630 (1997).

27. C. S. Holling. "Resilience and Stability of Ecological Systems," *Annual Review of Ecology and Systematics* 4 (1973).

28. "Total Crude Oil and Petroleum Products," US Energy Information Administration, 2012, www.eia.gov/dnav/pet/pet_cons_psup_dc_nus _mbblpd_a.htm; *Annual Energy Review*, US Energy Information Administration (Washington, DC: GPO, November 25, 2013), 69, 199.

29. *Monthly Energy Review*, US Energy Information Administration (Washington, DC: GPO, November 2013), 3.

30. "Monthly Oil Data Survey," International Energy Agency, December 13, 2013, www.iea.org/statistics/relatedsurveys/monthlyoildatasurvey.

31. "Risky Gas Drilling," Natural Resources Defense Council, www.nrdc.org/ energy/gasdrilling; "Tar Sands," National Wildlife Federation, www.nwf.org/ What-We-Do/Energy-and-Climate/Drilling-and-Mining/Tar-Sands.aspx.

32. J. R. Bartolino and W. L. Cunningham, "Ground-Water Depletion across the Nation" (Reston, VA: United States Geological Survey, 2003).

33. Barnett, T. P., and D. W. Pierce, "Sustainable Water Deliveries from the Colorado River in a Changing Climate," *Proceedings of the National Academy of Sciences of the United States of America* 106, no. 18 (2009): 7334–38.

34. Walter W. Immerzeel, Ludovicus P. H. van Beek, and Marc F. P. Bierkens, "Climate Change Will Affect the Asian Water Towers," *Science* 328, no. 5984 (June 11, 2010): 1382–85.

35. Andrew England, "Saudis to Phase out Wheat Production by 2016," *Financial Times*, April 11, 2008.

36. Lester R. Brown, *World on the Edge: How to Prevent Environmental and Economic Collapse* (New York: W. W. Norton, 2011), www.earth-policy.org, 21–33; M. Lagi, Yavni Bar-Yam, K. Z. Bertrand, and Yaneer Bar-Yam, "The Food Crises: A Quantitative Model of Food Prices Including Speculators and Ethanol Conversion" New England Complex Systems Institute. Submitted September 21, 2011, http://arxiv.org/abs/1109.4859.

37. Joel B. Smith, "Assessing Dangerous Climate Change through an Update of the Intergovernmental Panel on Climate Change (IPCC) 'Reasons for Concern,'" *Proceedings of the National Academy of Sciences of the United States of America* 106, no. 11 (2009): 4133–37.

38. Michael E. Mann, "Defining Dangerous Anthropogenic Interference," *Proceedings of the National Academy of Sciences of the United States of America* 106, no. 11 (2009): 4065–66.

39. A. P. Sokolov et al., "Probabilistic Forecast for Twenty-First-Century Climate Based on Uncertainties in Emissions (without Policy) and Climate Parameters," *Journal of Climate* 22, no. 19 (2009): 5175–204.

40. Kevin Anderson and Alice Bows, "Beyond 'Dangerous' Climate Change: Emission Scenarios for a New World," *Philosophical Transactions of the Royal Society A: Mathematical, Physical and Engineering Sciences* 369, no. 1934 (2011): 20–44.

41. New, Mark, et al., "Four Degrees and Beyond: The Potential for a Global Temperature Increase of Four Degrees and its Implications," special issue, *Philosophical Transactions of the Royal Society A* 369 no. 1934 (2011).

42. Paul Hawken, *Blessed Unrest: How the Largest Movement in the World Came into Being, and Why No One Saw It Coming* (New York: Viking, 2007).

43. David A. Lubin and Daniel C. Esty, "The Sustainability Imperative," *Harvard Business Review* 88, no. 5 (2010): 42–50.

3
Making the Transition

The First Steps

Building a sustainable library is, more than anything else, a practical undertaking, one ideally informed by clear thinking and a commitment to the values of our profession. It is also a hard task to start. Changes in our daily work routines, schedules, and software are hard to adjust to, and figuring out which changes to make is itself a complex undertaking, especially given the myriad other tasks demanding our attention. Given this, it makes sense for the first step in each library to be laying the groundwork by educating stakeholders about the importance of sustainability and the benefits it brings. In a time of shrinking budgets and staff, to be successful we need wide support and enthusiastic involvement. The key to that support is twofold. First, the process of educating staff, funders, patrons, and vendors needs to be inclusive and empowering. Handing people a brochure or book and expecting them to read it and understand it is not enough. There needs to be time and space for discussion as well as for debate. Creating a sustainable library is not as simple as creating a project team; it needs to go beyond that and create change in our basic work relationships and processes. And everyone needs to be invited to the table.

The good news is that, at this point in the transition, few library directors or boards are going to resist a staff-led sustainability committee. But the idea of sustainability does have serious opposition, and those opposing it need to feel welcomed into the process too, even if they choose not to participate. The second key to gaining support for the transition is to make sure that sustainability is understood broadly. Too often in libraries, sustainability initiatives do not go beyond internal greening programs, which are themselves valuable first steps. But by addressing the other two Es, equity and economy, we can build broader support and have wider relevance, while creating more successful sustainability programs.

There are many different steps individual library workers and librarians can undertake in their own libraries to start the conversation. The simplest is to host a reading group for staff interested in the issue. Libraries have a long history of "journal groups" and other sorts of in-house staff development activities, and this one is not that different. There are a number of excellent introductory texts in appendix C that could serve as the basis for a conversation about what the scientific facts are and the implications of those facts. By creating these kinds of groups, we create a forum for serious discussion and the beginnings of what can become an action-oriented committee looking at what changes can be made locally. These kinds of groups also give lower-level workers, workers who typically have less autonomy and less opportunity to have their voices heard, a context in which they can be influential and important. Part of managing well is giving all employees an opportunity to make their best contribution to the organization, and groups like this, ones that exist outside of the normal hierarchy, give staff opportunities to develop a personal stake in the success of the library, so they are powerful tools for improving morale and performance. They also do so with little cost. Increasing employee engagement and commitment through offering opportunities for low-cost staff development, increased autonomy, and greater participation in decision making is itself a step on the path toward a more sustainable library. Much like traditional journal clubs, sustainability-oriented reading groups encourage the self-organizing principles of systems to work for the benefit of the larger whole by strengthening the elements, in this case staff. Finally, and perhaps most important, reading groups change the flow of information within the library-as-system. By changing the flow of information to include sustainability information, the system itself is altered.

THE SUSTAINABILITY COMMITTEE

Reading groups are a good start, but they are only a start. To begin the work of making changes, we need to take advantage of our self-organizing abilities and change the way the system is structured so that sustainability can become a factor in how our organizations make decisions and evaluate results.

For most libraries, that means a committee of some sort, one empowered to contribute to important decisions, liaise with outside groups, and organize programming. Integrating the sustainability committee into decision making is key to transforming the library-as-system, but it does take time, a proactive stance by the committee, and support from all levels of the library hierarchy. However, by establishing an element within the library to take on the role of considering sustainability, it becomes possible to create a feedback loop based on information about sustainability and, thus, to begin the process of changing the way decisions are made.

Similarly, by making contacts with university offices of sustainability, local sustainability commissions, and vendor sustainability efforts, the library contributes to transforming the system through self-organization while making itself more sustainable in the process. Working with outside groups also ensures that the library has a seat at these important tables. Right now the library is too often overlooked by these groups and has no voice in their decisions. By getting a seat at the table, libraries gain opportunities to lead their communities and enhance their reputation. Library-led sustainability programming presents similar opportunities. Libraries are educational institutions first and foremost; by taking the initiative to create sustainability-themed programs for staff and patrons, libraries can improve information flow and increase community understanding about sustainability challenges, both local and global.

Determining who should serve on a sustainability committee and who should lead such a committee is tricky. Each library will have its own internal culture that will help to decide who joins. No one structure or plan can work for every library. That said, the Transition Town movement has a saying, one that makes sense for libraries too: The people sitting at the table are the right people. Whether the committee is nominated by library administrators or is self-selected, whoever turns up and participates is a good enough start. Just like at the reference desk, we must begin where we are and with whom we have. There are some strong arguments for keeping the committee outside of the traditional library hierarchy, though, and for doing what it takes to get frontline staff involvement and participation. The first is that any sustainability program is likely to recommend changes, the impacts of which are going to be felt most acutely by frontline staff. Whether it is changing toner brands, implementing a library composting program, or changing the way employees and patrons get to the library, those lowest on the hierarchy are going to welcome changes that they themselves have had a voice in making. Second, frontline staff know far more than others about the actual practices of the library. They are the ones who know when the lights are turned off, which recycling bins are used, how often the light bulbs are changed, and so on. Their input is crucial to the success of the sustainability effort.

It is also worthwhile to look outside the library for members. Is there someone in the Office of Sustainability or the Sustainability Commission who could offer valuable insight? What about local sustainability groups and campus student groups who have sustainability-based missions? Offering membership to these groups helps to build community support and strengthens ties between the library and its patrons. It is a healthy practice for any library committee, but especially sustainability committees which by their very nature will be change oriented, to welcome outside groups and invite wider participation. Wider participation does mean that the committee will need to begin a learning process not just about sustainability practices, but also about libraries and especially library values. This learning process is important and offers opportunities for library-wide programming while developing staff and enhancing community ties. It can also provide space for those on the committee to begin developing strong working relationships and talking openly about how the committee plans to do its work and what strategies will be most effective.

What about libraries where the administration is not supportive? It is a tough situation to be in but not a hopeless one. The good news is that, when sustainability is understood broadly, there are many different tacks to take to bring a reluctant administrator on board. The most obvious is cost savings. Many of the changes that lead to a more sustainable library, especially those related to ecology and economy, are likely to offer long-term financial benefits. From reducing paper waste to conserving water and energy, all the way to developing serials budget-control strategies, sustainability for libraries is in large part about saving and reallocating money and resources to fulfill the fundamental mission of the library. For those administrators not swayed by that aspect, there are other benefits too. Sustainability offers a leadership opportunity to the library, one that matches so well with its mission; we are unlikely to see another one come along in our lifetimes. By becoming a community leader in sustainability, the library can only enhance and improve its reputation and standing in the community. It also presents collection-strengthening, programming, and external-relationship-building opportunities, ones that can help to build better and stronger libraries. A major sustainability effort also offers administrators an opportunity to leave a valuable legacy to the library, one that will enhance their own reputation and, if done well, allow them to point to a significant accomplishment in a time of reduced budgets and shrinking staff. Finally, library administrators, like many people, may be stuck in the "it's not my problem and I can't fix it" mindset. The best solution to this mindset is education. If you have a strong enough relationship with your reluctant administrators, educate them. Offer them reading material and conversation. We are all together in this unfortunate predicament, and very few people want to be in it. By offering information from solution-oriented experts in the sustainability field, you might be able to sway them. Finally, do not be afraid to start small. Each step forward counts, and each step is valuable. There is no need or way to transform everything all at once. Instead, begin with the path of least resistance and make your way from there. Start where you can, and trust that over time you will get to where you want to be.

CONDUCTING A SUSTAINABILITY ASSESSMENT

Once a committee has been assembled and has completed some basic education about sustainability and libraries, it makes sense to move to a systematic assessment of the local library and its interface with various sustainability issues. Implementing any assessment program is challenging. Assessment takes time, energy, and considerable work across the library. Too often it can feel negative, like the library and its workers are being judged. It does not need to feel that way though. Each library has strengths and weaknesses. Sorting out what those are can help build a program that highlights strengths and provides a route for improving weaknesses. Different assessments also have different goals; the purpose of this assessment tool is to provide direction for those interested in improving the sustainability of a particular library. It is intended to be flexible and to identify areas where the library can improve its sustainability while also highlighting strengths. It is not intended to be scientific or to assign a grade. It is simply an evaluation and discussion tool. After conducting the assessment, it should be relatively straightforward to develop a sustainability plan that is based on the needs of each particular library, one that is both within reach and clearly actionable. It is not intended to offer a full look at the information ecosystem as a whole. We will come back to that in later chapters. The focus here is on what library staff can do within their own institutions, given the challenges the library is facing and the strengths it can build on. It can also help libraries to identify low-hanging fruit that can contribute to early successes. It is important not to underestimate the value of early success. The sooner a sustainability effort begins to show results, the stronger it will be going into more challenging issues. Those early successes, even small ones, help to build credibility and support, both of which are essential.

There are a large number of sustainability assessment tools out there; however, the one offered here is the first created specifically for use by libraries. It draws on the Association for Sustainability in Higher Education's STARS Assessment program, the How Green Is Your Library assessment offered by Sam Mulford and Ned Himmel, as well as the considerable body of research into sustainability assessment and library assessment. It is an integrated assessment tool, meaning that it considers the triple bottom line of ecology, equity, and economy.[1] It includes four parts: a general section and then a section for each of the three Es. The first part is offered below, and the others are in subsequent chapters. A complete version is found in appendix A. The overall goal of the assessment is to take users through a system-level analysis of their library, one that focuses on the sustainability of the library as whole. It is suitable for different kinds of libraries, but not every library will need to answer all of it. Rather, sustainability committees and others considering using it should feel comfortable adapting it to their own needs. There is no grade or qualitative judgment; instead, it offers a framework for discussion and for developing a library-specific plan of action, one that offers ideas for library administrators and for library workers who wish to do what they can within their own institutions.

The first part of the assessment tool is intended to give the committee a broad overview of the local sustainability landscape. Each item in the first part offers a series of questions designed to help sustainability committees or individuals interested in making their own libraries more sustainable determine how much education will need to be offered to local stakeholders and what relationships need to be built. When completed along with the other parts, it should suggest actions the committee can take to develop a strong sustainability plan and should help the committee identify a starting point for its efforts.

THE ASSESSMENT TOOL—PART 1

1. The sustainability committee

Is there one? If not, does one make sense for this library? Who should serve on the committee? How can it include members from across the library hierarchy and system? How often should it plan to meet, and what are its immediate goals? Who from outside the library should it include? What about branch libraries? How does it fit into the larger library committee structure? Does the committee have a written mission or vision? What is the process for setting objectives and informing the library about its activities?

2. Support for sustainability initiatives

Does the committee or person completing the assessment believe that the library administration is supportive of transitioning to a more sustainable model? What about the city or university administration? Does the city or university participate in a sustainability assessment? What do the results of that assessment say? Are library staff members generally supportive? If not, how can the committee work to build support? What about patrons? Is the community in general engaged with sustainability issues?

3. Relationships with outside sustainability groups

What does the local sustainability community look like? What groups should the library reach out to both to support the efforts of others and to get support for changes in the library? Who are the key players in the local sustainability community? Are there regular meetings of a sustainability commission or other official group that the library should join or attend? Is there a farmers market, Transition Town group, or other local sustainability initiative the library should consider supporting with programming or collection building?

4. Sustainability programming and collections

What kinds of sustainability programming does the library already do? Does the library have an Earth Day program or host other kinds of programming with an environmental theme? What about the collection? Does it need updating or broadening? For public libraries, does it include the kinds of practical information needed for families and local businesses considering things like alternative energy or teaching children about climate change? For academic libraries, does it include the major theoretical works on sustainability issues as well as work on sustainability in higher education? Look at WorldCat and compare local holdings to the range of titles available on sustainability themes. Look at the bibliography provided and which titles might be valuable additions to the local collection.

5. Sustainability plan

Does the university or city have an existing sustainability plan? How does the library fit into this plan, and how can that plan be incorporated into a library plan? What is the vision for a sustainable future, and how can the library contribute to moving toward that vision?

The information gathered for this part of the assessment should help everyone on the committee, or help the individuals conducting the assessment if no committee has been formed, better understand the local context for sustainability. Is the environment welcoming of such efforts, or is more education needed? The answer to this question is absolutely crucial. Some libraries will be in a place where there is a well-developed local community dedicated to sustainability. These libraries are going to be able to take more advanced steps toward transition than libraries that find themselves at the cutting edge of their communities. The good news is that you have found where you are and what you can do in your local area to effect change.

CREATING A SUSTAINABILITY PLAN

When the entire sustainability assessment has been conducted, it is time to begin formulating a sustainability plan. A plan will provide structure and direction for sustainability efforts. It will also help to define success and allow the committee to point to a list of accomplishments. It will likely take a period of months or even a year, depending on the size of the library, to create such a plan. However, the work will be well worth the effort because, at the end of it, the library will have a clear way forward. A sample plan is offered in appendix B, but it is only an example. The plan can be as simple or as complex as your particular institution needs or is ready for. Small libraries can have plans that match their nimbleness and budgets, and large libraries can build plans that will work for their more complex administrative structure and larger budgets. Similarly, libraries in places that are deeply committed to sustainability can have plans that match the ambition of the local community. Libraries in places where sustainability is not yet a local priority can have plans focusing on simpler goals or goals that focus on the area likely to get the most support, for example, budget control. No matter the details of the plan, there are certain elements that will help to create stronger plans for every kind of library. The first priority for a sustainability plan should be to tie it into the existing mission and values of the library and the parent organization. The sustainability plan is a working document, but it is also a communication tool, one that should reflect the existing image of the library and parent institution while tying into its current themes and goals. There are a few ways to do this. The simplest is to take the language from the mission or vision and see what parts can be easily adapted. For example, if the current vision statement talks about the importance of literacy, tie into that by including environmental literacy as part of the sustainability plan. You can also build on existing concepts in the vision or mission. If the mission talks about service to the community, build on that by discussing serving the larger community through more sustainable practices.

SUSTAINABILITY VISION

University Library seeks to support the mission of the University and the Library by becoming a sustainability leader on the campus and within the library community. University Library will accomplish this by focusing our efforts on enhancing the environmental literacy of the campus and community through programming and collections, developing new green practices for our daily work, enhancing the scholarly communication system through the development of an institutional repository while encouraging and supporting open access initiatives, and putting into practice our commitment to equality and democracy by building a diverse, equitably compensated, and empowered staff.

Second, a plan should have clear goals and measurable objectives derived from the assessment. It should also have realistic goals, ones that are attainable in your particular library. There is an entire literature on goal and objective setting that is well worth familiarizing yourself with, especially if this is the first time you have led a major project. The process of goal setting is complicated and requires a variety of skill sets, most importantly the ability to lead effective meetings and solicit meaningful feedback from diverse audiences. The example below offers a sample of an effective sustainability goal with measurable objectives and action items.

SAMPLE SUSTAINABILITY GOAL

Goal: University Library will reduce its carbon footprint.

Objective: University Library will schedule an energy audit with Physical Plant and will then examine the results and add objectives as needed.

Action Item: Schedule audit by January 12.

Objective: University Library will encourage staff and patrons to use alternative transportation to get to the library.

Action Item: Contact University Office of Sustainability to inquire about existing incentive programs for staff.

Action Item: Gather relevant bus/train schedules and make them available.

Action Item: Communicate with department heads and other managers to suggest that they work with staff to ensure that schedules are compatible with public transport.

Action Item: Develop a list of volunteers who are willing to assist if someone needs emergency transport during the day, for example, because a child is sick.

Action Item: Contact Physical Plant and ask that existing bike rack be moved to a more convenient location and repainted.

The plan should also include checkpoints for the future and lay out a process for retiring objectives and action items. Goals can also be retired but should not need to be changed frequently. By keeping the document in a wiki, course management system, or other easy to access and change format, committee members can note completed action items and propose next-step objectives.

A good plan will also address the role and membership of the sustainability committee itself. Libraries are so different in their cultures that it is hard to suggest any hard and fast rules, however there are a few things to consider. In larger libraries, where most work is done through committees, it is important to define the relationship of the sustainability committee to other committees. Is it an approval committee? A suggestive committee? Does it report to the director, to the assistant director, or to some other administrator? Working these things out and putting them down on paper is a good exercise and will help to ensure that, as the membership changes over time, the committee can stay true to its function. It is also a good idea to lay out in the plan who will serve on the committee, for how long, and how they will be selected. Committee leadership is also worth clarifying. Who will lead the committee and for how long? How will new leaders be selected, and who will approve their appointments? For some libraries the answer to these questions will be quite obvious: the director. Other places may have different structures and processes in place. Sorting out what those are is an important step in solidifying the role of the committee and ensuring its future success.

Finally, a short sustainability plan is a good thing. Keeping the introduction brief, the goals realistic, and the objectives manageable will contribute to a successful transition. It will also reduce the amount of backlash and help others who might be intimidated by the transition. The easier and more achievable the immediate goals are, the more success the committee will enjoy. Small and early successes build to long-term and major successes over time. Staying on course for the long term is far more important and a far more effective strategy than taking giant leaps. This is not say that if you are in a place and at a time where giant leaps are possible you shouldn't take them, but libraries are conservative institutions. Big, bold initiatives are few and far between and a fair number of them end up in the waste bin. Small, measurable changes sustained over time are a more reasonable strategy for most of us. Especially when our ultimate goals are so very audacious.

NOTE

1. Sam McBane Mulford and Ned A. Himmel, *How Green Is My Library?* (Santa Barbara, CA: Libraries Unlimited, 2010); *Stars Technical Manual*, Association for the Advancement of Sustainability in Higher Education, October 2013, www.aashe.org/files/documents/STARS/2.0/stars_2.0.1_technical_manual.pdf.

PART II

Building a Sustainable Library

4
Ecology

library greening programs are a great place to start a library sustainability effort. They can save money, they tend to have wide support, and they are an effective means to create the kinds of changes that lead a library down an increasingly sustainable path. There are a number of excellent books on the subject in print; this chapter can only serve as an introduction to the topic. Because the topic is so big, further reading will be necessary as your library begins drawing up its plan. This chapter also does not address what to do if you are in the enviable position of influencing a major renovation or an entirely new building. Books and other resources for those lucky librarians and library workers are listed in appendix C. Instead, this chapter is intended to help the vast majority of us who cannot build a new building or conduct a major renovation and so must restrict our efforts to making changes in our work processes and purchasing decisions. The good news is that there are many changes we can make without significant expenditures and without having to retrofit or replace our buildings. These are changes we can make quite simply that will have a major impact on bringing our libraries toward sustainability. They will also contribute toward creating an environment that is friendly to other changes by building momentum through early success. The stronger a new program or initiative can be at the start, the more momentum will build, and things that used to seem impossible will become possible.

DECARBONIZING

The carbon and other pollution problems embedded in the larger information ecosystem, ones whose solutions require collective action, are discussed in later chapters. However, it is worth considering those for a moment before we move on to the individual library level. Reducing direct energy use, through both electricity and transportation, is the main way that individual libraries can contribute to reducing carbon; however, those changes represent only part of the actual carbon emissions created by our current information ecosystem. Significant carbon emissions also come from shipping, forest loss for paper, mining of minerals for technologies like computers and printers, and the operation of the large server operations that most of our content vendors run on our behalf. Environmental groups like Smart 2020 report that cloud computing and other technology industry emissions are about 830 million tons of CO_2 equivalent, which includes CO_2 and other greenhouse gases, per year.[1] Given this, it is worth taking a close look at the print versus electronic question in the context of carbon emissions. Most librarians tend to assume the electronic sources are always better for the environment, but that is not true.[2] Gard and Keoleian looked at this question and found that, in fact, it is only true when most people are getting to the library via car.[3] If you take transportation out of the mix, which many residential schools and large city libraries can do, print materials come out better than electronics. Of course, few people want to return to an exclusively print library, which means that the challenges presented by electronic materials and services need to be solved. As major consumers of these services and products, changing this should be a high priority for the library community. It is not, however, a problem that individual libraries can solve. Rather, it is one that requires collective action on the part of the profession.

The changes suggested in this chapter are local changes intended to help individual libraries reduce the amount of greenhouse gases they produce directly. Separating decarbonizing strategies from other issues highlights the importance of decarbonizing and allows libraries to track the process of reducing their carbon footprint. Decarbonizing is particularly important because climate change is such a serious problem and the changes we need to make so deep and urgent. Fortunately, there are many small adjustments (and some large ones) libraries can undertake to reduce their footprints. Other changes are important too, so keeping in mind one of the basic tenets of sustainability, the idea of interrelated systems, an effective strategy is one that combines decarbonizing strategies with ones for reducing landfill waste, water usage, and harmful chemicals. It is also important to weigh the impacts of any change against the so-called triple bottom line of ecology, economy, and equity. For example, while seeking LEED certification, a green building program may very well be good for the environment if it pushes a project so far over budget that it becomes economically unviable; then it is not a sustainable solution. As you conduct your assessment and then begin building a library sustainability plan, keep this in mind. The goal is to create a plan that actually works and that can be implemented, at least in part, with resources on hand.

To begin the process of decarbonizing your library, it is important to understand what processes generate carbon and how much carbon your library generates. The process for doing this is known as carbon footprinting. Carbon footprinting evolved from the idea of the ecological footprint, or carrying capacity, first developed by William Rees.[4] The basic idea is to determine how much of the Earth's resources are being used to sustain a particular person, business, or even a whole country. Ecological footprinting has been applied to many different types of activities at many different levels. Its main advantage is that it offers a simple way to understand what is in fact a very complicated, and often nontransparent, system. Because ecological footprinting considers both direct and indirect use of resources, it shows hidden impacts. Carbon footprinting is similar but focused specifically on carbon emissions. A carbon footprint analysis usually considers electricity use, both what kinds and how efficiently it is used, and transportation choices. For manufacturing industries, carbon footprint analysis also reviews the emission of other greenhouse gases, forest and land degradation, and other carbon sources.

It is a complex process, one that really does require an expert to conduct properly. If you have a local sustainability commission or office of sustainability, working with them to see what resources are available to conduct a carbon footprint analysis is a good first start. It is possible, especially if you are at a university, that such an assessment has been conducted for the institution as a whole. Reading that analysis is also good place to start. For libraries that do not have access to this type of resource, which is probably most, the good news is that there are other options for determining carbon emissions and how to reduce them. Almost all energy utilities offer audits designed to help businesses and households reduce their energy usage, which almost always means reducing their carbon footprint as well. Calling your local company and setting one up is a good idea. Energy audits are often free and include a helpful list of energy saving tips that can be added to the sustainability plan and then implemented. Aside from energy, the other major source of carbon emissions for individual libraries is transportation for both staff and patrons. The fewer people getting to your library in a personal car, the smaller the library's carbon footprint will be. Transportation is a particularly good area to focus on, because there is much a library can do to influence how people get to the library.

To return to our sustainability assessment, there are a number of data gathering activities that should be the first step in determining which decarbonizing strategies make sense for your library. Some libraries will find low-hanging fruit in electricity usage and efficiency, while others will find transportation offers more opportunities. The questions below are designed to help you figure that out. Each section is followed by an explanation of which choices represent stronger decarbonizing strategies and ideas for how to implement better policies.

THE ASSESSMENT TOOL—PART 2.1: ELECTRICITY

Electricity Usage in the Library

1. Measurement

Has your library had an energy audit or other carbon footprint assessment done? Is there an institutional sustainability assessment available that might contain that information? How much electricity does the library use each year, each month? Are there discernible patterns in usage, i.e., higher in the summer? How is the electricity that the library uses generated? (This information should be readily available on the local utility's website.)

Determining how much energy your institution uses is an important step because it provides a baseline to measure efforts going forward. Not all libraries will have access to this information though, especially academic libraries who get their power through the larger campus system. Talk to your office of sustainability or physical plant to see what they can offer. An energy audit, conducted either by the local utility or your physical plant is highly recommended as part of this assessment. By having an expert come in and review your energy use and make site specific recommendations, you should be able to understand your strengths and weaknesses. Because the service is often free and leads to cost savings, there is really no reason not to pursue it. Finally, by understanding how your electricity is generated, you will know whether electricity is something you need to closely manage or if, for a lucky few, something that is not currently generating a large amount of carbon. Most power in the United States is generated by burning coal, however some comes from nuclear, hydroelectric, and renewable sources. If you are in a coal-fired library, efficiency should be a high goal because it is likely to have a large impact on your carbon footprint. Libraries who get their power from other sources should, of course, still work on conservation, but for reasons other than carbon emissions.

THE ASSESSMENT TOOL—PART 2.1: ELECTRICITY (continued)

2. Lighting

Determine how many different kinds lighting your library has, i.e., outside, overhead, task etc. What kinds of bulbs are currently being used and how many? Is the library currently using any solar, LED, or CFL bulbs? What about timers in the stacks or motion sensitive lights? Are all lights turned off at night? Is the security lighting adequate or excessive?

Most libraries use a wide range of lighting, including outside sign and building lighting, parking lot lighting, overhead lights inside, task lighting of various sorts, and emergency lighting. The one common refrain on saving energy through lighting is that spending money upfront to purchase better bulbs and fixtures saves money in the long run. Solar, LED, and CFL cost more to buy but less to run, however over time the energy savings more than makes up for it, as you can see in the chart. (See table 4.1.) Outside lighting can be done with solar energy and many of these fixtures are not very expensive and last a very long time. Inside, most libraries use some kind of florescent overhead lighting. Changing these to T-8 bulbs can offer considerable energy savings. Installing motion sensors and timers can also be a good, low cost, way to save energy. Bathrooms, stacks, and other areas that are not in constant use are good candidates for timers and motion sensors. Finally, educating staff to shut down computers and work-space lighting at the end of the day and when not in use offers a virtually free way to save energy. This does require managers to be supportive. Comments like, "Oh, your light was off so I thought you went home," need to be eliminated so that employees do not leave their light on as a way to say, "I'm here!"

THE ASSESSMENT TOOL—PART 2.1: ELECTRICITY (continued)

3. Heating and Cooling

What is the current schedule for cleaning the filter and is it actually followed? What about insulation? Would the building benefit from better insulation and window treatments? What temperature is the building maintained at in summer, winter? What is the library's policy on space heaters? Can this be changed to minimize energy usage while still maintaining the comfort of patrons and staff? Does the employee dress code allow appropriate seasonal clothing in the summer?

Heating and cooling will represent a significant part of any library's energy budget. Unfortunately, changing an HVAC system is usually expensive. If you are in a position to pursue a new system, be sure to review the list of

TABLE 4.1

Lighting and Energy Savings

	LED	CFL	Incandescent
Lightbulb projected life span	50,000 hours	10,000 hours	1,200 hours
Watts per bulb (equivalent 60 watts)	10	14	60
Cost per bulb	$35.95	$3.95	$1.25
kWh of electricity used over 50,000 hours	500	700	3,000
Cost of electricity ($.10 per kWh)	$50	$70	$300
Bulbs needed for 50,000 hours' use	1	5	42
Equivalent 50,000 hours' bulb expense	$35.95	$19.75	$52.50
Total cost for 50,000 hours	**$85.75**	**$89.75**	**$352.50**

resources for new buildings and renovations. There are resources there that can help you make a wise decision. For those of us who must make the best of what we have, there are things librarians and library workers can do to improve the efficiency of the existing system. Checking and cleaning the filter according the manufacturers recommendations are important and will improve the efficiency of the system. Insulation is another low-cost option. Window films, blown in insulation, and sealing cracks and other openings will reduce your need for heating and cooling by helping your building maintain its temperature. Lowering the thermostat in the winter and raising it in the summer can also work for some libraries. Generally, 68°F in the winter and 72 in the summer represents a good compromise between comfort and efficiency. Finally, space heaters are a large energy drain. Banning them or purchasing only very efficient ones is a good policy. Another low cost option that may help reduce heating and cooling costs is reviewing the dress code. Are employees permitted to wear seasonable clothing? Allowing shorts in the summer and not requiring jackets can help employees to be comfortable and reduce the need for air conditioning, as can ensuring that each employee has a place they can store a sweater or jacket if it is chilly. As Sam Mulford and Ned Himmel point out in *How Green is My Library?* this works best when management models seasonal clothing themselves to ensure that employees feel confident in their wardrobe choices.[5]

THE ASSESSMENT TOOL—PART 2.1: ELECTRICITY (continued)

4. Computers and Printers

Are the computers and printers turned off every night? Are they set up to default to an energy-saving mode when not in use? Has the library chosen Energy Star Rated machines?

TABLE 4.2

Energy Star Computer Savings

How Your Computers Are Used	Estimated Lifetime (4 yrs.) Savings per Desktop Computer	
	If you pay $.11 per kWh	*If you pay $.18 per kWh*
We typically leave our computers on nights and weekends	$88	$144
We typically turn our computers off every night	$24	$40
We will activate power management settings on the new computers but did not do so on the old computers	$216	$352

Source: www.energystar.gov/index.cfm?fuseaction=find_a_product.showProductGroup&pgw_code=CO

I had worked at my library for two years before I realized that my student assistants were only turning off the computers on the first floor. Turning off computers and other electronic devices like printers, scanners, and copiers at the end of the day and keeping them in energy-saver mode the rest of the time they are not in use is a simple and cost-free way to save energy. Buying Energy Star Rated machines is another one. The chart below shows the savings choosing an Energy Star computer can bring. Given how many computers libraries have these days, the savings add up quickly. (See table 4.2.) Printers and scanners too can be Energy Star Rated, so be sure to consider that when making purchasing decisions.

Electricity is one prong of a two-pronged decarbonizing strategy for libraries; transportation represents the other side. The questions below take you through the process of evaluating how people get to your library and how you get around to your patrons.

THE ASSESSMENT TOOL—PART 2.2: TRANSPORTATION AND THE LIBRARY

1. Employees

How do most employees get to work? If employees aren't using public transport, why not? Are many employees carpooling and if not, why? What are the local public transportation choices? Does the library offer any incentives to encourage public transportation or carpooling? What about biking employees? Are there easily accessible bike racks? Is there a shower or other facility for employees to use if they need to refresh after biking to work? Does the library have a telecommuting policy and is it used? When employees travel out of town for conferences and other events, are they encouraged to use trains instead of airplanes or cars?

A simple SurveyMonkey or Google form can be used to collect this information. It is a good idea to use the form not only to solicit information, but also ask what ideas employees have for encouraging public transportation use, carpooling, biking, and walking. For libraries where most employees are using a car, changing this will offer a good decarbonizing solution. In areas where the public transportation system is strong, libraries have many different options for encouraging its use. Working with the local transportation agency to make sure there is a nearby stop is a good first step. Libraries can also negotiate employee discounts for bus and train passes. Many city governments and large universities already have such discounts, so be sure to check and see if one already exists and promote it if it does. Employee schedules and regular meeting times can also be adjusted to ensure that as many people as possible are able to use public transport. Employees who do not work a typical 8–5 schedule are particularly good candidates for schedule reviews. Sometimes something as simple as adjusting an ending time by 15 minutes can be the difference between public transportation being a viable option or not.

For libraries without a strong local public transportation system, there are other options. Carpooling can be a good option for many employees. There are a number of easy steps libraries can take to encourage employees to carpool, ranging from schedule changes for both employees and meetings, setting up a plan for employees who need emergency transportation during the day, such as for a sick child, and helping employees to organize carpools by providing sign-up sheets and a time for discussion.[6] Encouraging walking and biking is a bit harder because they both rely on employees already living nearby. However, there a few things libraries can do to make it easier. Provide secure bike racks in a convenient location and a place for employees to wash up if possible. Make sure the dress code is not so strict that walking and biking require a full change of clothes for employees. Also, be sure that employees have a place to store bike helmets, umbrellas, and winter clothing. Telecommuting is another strategy libraries can use to reduce employee car use. If your library does not have a telecommuting policy, creating one and encouraging its use can be a step in the right direction. Employees who travel out of town to conferences and meetings should be encouraged to take the train when possible. Trains are far less carbon emitting than either personal cars or airplanes.[7] They can also be cheaper. Encourage train use by allowing employees the extra time needed, using travel agents that book train travel, and adding a policy to the employee handbook indicating that train travel is preferred when possible.

THE ASSESSMENT TOOL—PART 2.2:
TRANSPORTATION AND THE LIBRARY (continued)

2. Patrons

How do most patrons get to the library? Consider a survey (an in-building one) to get this information if it isn't already apparent. Is the library well situated from public transport stops and if not, is this a fixable barrier? Are schedules and other information about public transportation options readily available at the library? Is there an existing relationship between the library and the transportation agency that can be built on for cross promotion? Are programs and other events timed to make it easy for patrons to use public transportation? Is the library accessible to walkers and bicyclists? Are there easy landscaping or parking lot changes (like adding crosswalks and bike racks) that can be made? What else could the library do to make itself less car friendly and more friendly to alternative transportation choices?

Changing the way patrons get to the library, short of building a new building in a new place, is tough. However, there are a few things libraries can do short of that to make it easier for patrons to make other transportation choices. Make sure that the library is on public transportation routes. Is the route to the library clearly marked on bus and train schedules? Are the online mapping programs providing accurate public transport, walking, and biking directions. If not, see if that can be changed. Make schedules and fare information easily accessible to patrons and advertise how easy it is to get to the library on the bus or train. If it is not easy to get to the library, see if that can be changed. Schedule programs and other events to make it easy for patrons to use public transportation to both get there and leave the event. Build a relationship with your local transportation agency and develop cross promotional ideas. To make the library more accessible to walkers and bicyclists, create safe passage through parking lots and make sure the bike racks are easy to find and safe to use. If there is a troublesome intersection that would benefit from a crosswalk, request one. It might take a long time to get one put in, but asking will at least bring the matter to the attention of people who can change it. Finally, look carefully around your particular library and at your particular set of transportation options and be creative. Is there another choice that would work for your library? If so, pursue it.

THE ASSESSMENT TOOL—PART 2.2:
TRANSPORTATION AND THE LIBRARY (continued)

3. Library Owned Vehicles

How many vehicles does the library own, and for what purpose are they used? Are they scheduled to be replaced soon, or are they likely to be in use for the foreseeable future? Are they all gasoline, or does the library own a hybrid or other alternative fuel vehicle? Is there any support for purchasing a new hybrid or alternative fuel vehicle at this time? Consider the existing uses of the vehicles. Can the miles driven be reduced by combining trips or replacing some with other transportation alternatives? If the vehicles are used only to travel a small distance, could a golf cart or other electric vehicle be used instead? What about couriers used by local and regional consortiums? Could the library advocate for those services to be run using alternative fuel vehicles?

Bookmobiles and other library owned vehicles represent a significant investment. Using them wisely and, when the opportunity is there, choosing hybrid vehicles over traditional diesel or gasoline powered vehicles, can lead to a substantial carbon footprint reduction. New hybrid bookmobiles also offer a good opportunity to pursue grant money. Of course, not every library is in a position to buy a new bookmobile or replace its other vehicles. If your library is in that category, as most will be, you can still work on reducing your vehicles' carbon footprint by reducing and combining trips, keeping the tires inflated, and reducing idling when possible. If you use a local or regional courier as part of a consortial lending program or for ILL, advocate for those vehicles to be hybrid powered.

BEYOND CARBON

Carbon reduction is one aspect of a multi-pronged strategy to reduce the environmental impact individual libraries have, but there are other steps libraries can and should take as well. The next part of the assessment looks at other impacts that individual libraries have on the environment and how better practices can reduce these impacts. Like the decarbonizing sections above, the focus here is on what individual libraries can do without building a new building or incurring other large costs.

THE ASSESSMENT TOOL—PART 3: OTHER GREEN PRACTICES

1. Solid Waste

Does your library have an effective recycling program in place for paper, plastic, and metals? Are bins available, accessible, and actually used by both patrons and staff? What about food waste and compostables? Is a library compost pile a workable idea? If not, is there a gardener on staff or a community garden that would welcome the library's compostable waste? What about batteries and printer cartridges? Does the library offer both staff and the public disposal bins for these? Finally, for most libraries, withdrawn books are a very large percentage of the waste stream. Consider your current procedures for these materials. Are you selling what you can and donating where possible? Do you have a contract with a book recycler for these items?

Between newspapers, magazines, publishers' catalogs, withdrawn books and media items, plus printer paper waste and used (and reused) shipping supplies, libraries throw out quite a bit of trash. The good news is that most of that waste is some form of paper and therefore easily recyclable. Be sure you have adequate bins and that the signage matches the needs of your local recycler. If your library does not already offer proper disposal of batteries and printer cartridges, consider adding this service. For most libraries, this will be a low- or no-cost public service. Talk to your office of sustainability, campus physical plant, or municipal waste handlers to see about getting bins for these items. If the service is not available from your campus or community yet, there are many companies who will be happy to work with you to set up a program. Search for "battery recycling" to find one in your area. Withdrawn materials are a bit more complicated to properly dispose of because the volume is often large but sporadic. Many libraries hold regular used book sales to dispose of some materials; if yours does not, look into working with your Friends of the Library group to set up a small cart of books for sale. Donating unwanted materials through organizations like Better World Books is also a good option. Some books will still need to be thrown out though, either because they are outdated or so worn they are no longer usable. Because these materials cannot be recycled through most campus and municipal programs, recycling these materials through a book recycler is a good and very low-cost option for most libraries.

THE ASSESSMENT TOOL—PART 3:
OTHER GREEN PRACTICES (continued)

2. E-Waste

How does your library currently dispose of e-waste, i.e., old computers, printers, and miscellaneous electronics? Are materials currently being properly reused or recycled? If not, check with your local waste materials handler or office of sustainability to see what options exist in your area and how your library can begin recycling these items.

E-waste is a serious and rapidly growing problem, but one that is also widely recognized and is being actively improved across the country. Because e-waste contains both toxins and rare materials that are recyclable, computers, televisions, and other electronics should never be just thrown out. Throwing them out contaminates municipal landfills and potentially waterways as well. It is also likely illegal because most municipalities have regulations prohibiting toxic materials from being disposed of in local landfills. If there is no good process already in place, investigate local options through your municipal waste handlers or your office of sustainability. If neither of these has a program in place, setting one up for your library is simple but unlikely to be cost free. Begin by researching local companies that specialize in e-waste handling to see what options are available for your library's e-waste. Be sure to choose a reputable recycler, one that has been certified under the E-Stewards program. E-Stewards certified recyclers have agreed to adhere to high standards of both worker safety and environmental responsibility. Because so much e-waste ends up in large landfills in the developing world where it is processed using child labor, it is especially important from a sustainability standpoint to use a certified recycler who processes e-waste safely.

THE ASSESSMENT TOOL—PART 3:
OTHER GREEN PRACTICES (continued)

3. Water Usage

How much water does your library use and what does it use it for? Water bills and your local water company's website should provide this information. Are green areas appropriately landscaped for your climate? Do any of the taps drip or toilets run? Are low flow toilets and automated faucets a possibility? Are there other water hungry activities specific to your library and, if so, is the water being used carefully?

The largest use of water for most individual libraries is for landscaping. Landscaping your library with native plants and trees, ones suited to your climate and your local rainfall, can significantly reduce water usage. Libraries in arid areas should consider xeriscaping as a water conserving option. Relandscaping, while not free, can also offer good programming and community relations building opportunities. By working with a local community garden or a local gardener who has been certified through your USDA extension office, you can turn the project into a learning opportunity for the whole community while also building ties with other organizations. Native plants and trees can also often be purchased more cheaply than traditional landscape plants, especially if bought in the fall.

THE ASSESSMENT TOOL—PART 3:
OTHER GREEN PRACTICES (continued)

4. Buying Green

Has your library made the switch to using post-consumer content recycled paper? Are your cleaning supplies free of hazardous chemicals, including phosphates and petrochemical-free? What about your shipping supplies, especially for interlibrary loan? Is the library choosing recycled products and reusing where possible?

The environment is not going to be saved through shopping, however choosing products that are manufactured in an environmentally friendly way, are not directly harmful to the environment, and are easily disposed of is a step in the right direction. Be wary of information from manufacturers that reads like advertising copy and promotes the "greenness" of their products. So-called greenwashing, overhyping the environmental benefits of a product to sell more of it, is pervasive. Read critically and rely on independent external programs, ones like GreenSeal and GoodGuide, for reviews and information about the sustainability of products.

NOTES

1. The Climate Group, *Smart 2020: Enabling the Low Carbon Economy in the Information Age*, ed. GeSI (Creative Commons, 2008).
2. David L. Gard and Gregory A. Keoleian, "Digital Versus Print: Energy Performance in the Selection and Use of Scholarly Journals," *Journal of Industrial Ecology* 6, no. 2 (2003): 115–32.
3. Ibid., 129.

4. William E. Rees, "Ecological Footprints and Appropriated Carrying Capacity: What Urban Economics Leaves Out," *Environment and Urbanization* 4, no. 2 (1992): 121–30.
5. Sam McBane Mulford and Ned A. Himmel, *How Green Is My Library?* (2010), 123
6. Mulford and Himmel, *How Green Is My Library?*.
7. "Planes, Trains, or Automobiles: Travel Choices for a Smaller Carbon Footprint," *Science Daily* (June 17, 2013).

5
Economy

L ibrary greening programs are easier than confronting the economic and equity aspects of sustainability. However, to create the kind of change that we need within our institutions, it is important to address the other two Es as well. A sustainability committee cannot possibly do it all alone though. Collaboration and cooperation across departments are going to be necessary, which is why having a diverse sustainability committee is so important. The wider the representation on the sustainability committee, both vertically and horizontally, the easier the work will be for the committee. That said, many of the suggestions laid out in the following chapters are far beyond what one committee can or should address. Instead, the goal of the sustainability committee should be to collect and disseminate information and bring the many diverse areas where the library is working on building a more sustainable library under one plan. Work with the relevant departments to form a set of goals and objectives that meet their current needs and take into account their current resources. And remember that achieving those goals and objectives is going to be up to them. The sustainability committee can help by marshaling resources for those departments, building support with key stakeholders, and ensuring that credit is given to the department making the changes. Let them enjoy their victories while you promote the success of the Sustainability Plan in helping them to achieve those victories. With that in mind, consider the suggestions below and think about what would work at your institution. Not all items are sensible or achievable for every library and that is fine. Focus on your institution and what will lead to its transformation toward a more sustainable library.

The economic sustainability of libraries is at risk from multiple directions, ranging from a reduced investment in public services to the ongoing price increases levied by publishers to the need to replace expensive technology on a regular schedule. Despite these pressures though, there is much librarians can do within their own institutions to build and preserve healthy library budgets. And building and preserving healthy library budgets are an absolutely crucial part of any sustainability effort. Without economic sustainability, libraries, both individually and collectively, cannot possibly continue to exist as thriving institutions. Money, no matter how little we like thinking about it or being engaged with the world of finance or taxation, is what allows us to build strong collections, provide needed services, run excellent programs, and keep our doors open. All librarians and library workers need to concern themselves with the economic health of their institution and do what they can to ensure that money is spent wisely and that those who hold the purse strings know the value of our work.

The core problem is that libraries are facing reductions in the amount of funding we receive while our expenses continue to increase. This trend is well documented in the literature, for both public and academic libraries. Both problems, however, are rooted in the same trend—the ongoing effort to expand the reach of the market and reduce social services. Schools, public housing, and benefits for the poor have all seen a similar decline in their funding over the past 30 years. John Buschmann documents this decline beautifully in his work *Dismantling the Public Sphere*. There he calls attention to the ongoing and largely successful attempts to defund public services and increase the power of the market through privatization.[1] The impact of this project on libraries has been severe, resulting in a move to reduce hours, services, and collections. The recent recession and weak recovery have only enhanced this problem and led to an even more acute crisis for many libraries. At the same time, we are also struggling with the entrance of large, very powerful, corporate interests into the scholarly communications sector. The rise of multinational corporations who take very large profits, companies like Informa (Taylor and Francis), Wiley, and of course, Elsevier, has radically changed what was once a largely nonprofit scholarly communication system and libraries are only beginning to develop effective resistance strategies.[2] Fortunately, librarians are in a good position to lead a transformation of the scholarly communications system and so preserve library budgets and increase access for our patrons. Leading this transformation is one of the most important ways that we can contribute toward building a more sustainable model for the future.

The challenge of reducing materials costs, a necessary tactic, is one that requires political mobilization and will only be addressed briefly in this chapter; for more on that see Part 3. Instead, the Sustainability Assessment will focus on how libraries can work within their institutions to transform the structure of scholarly publishing and work at the local level for other systemic changes in the overall information system. Beyond the information system too, there is also a role for libraries to play in their own communities as consumers who can contribute to the economic health of the local community. Developing the local economy as much as possible and spending library dollars locally and regionally are important contributions that libraries can make to their local community and its long-term economic health. Both strategies, transforming the information ecosystem and supporting the local economy, are important in transitioning to a more sustainable world and both are areas where individual libraries and librarians can make a large impact on the overall transition to a more sustainable world.

This first section is intended to help libraries look at their local environment and identify areas where they can help to both build support for increased funding and support their local scholars as they transition to an open access model. At the same time, it will also help libraries to identify strategies to use going forward that will help regain the control over budgets that was lost in the "big deal" era.

LIBRARY BUDGETS

One of the primary paths to the long-term sustainability of libraries is the creation of a resilient budget. Resilience is defined as "the capacity of a system to absorb disturbance and still retain its basic function and structure."[3] For libraries, creating resilience in the budget is a challenge. However, by working both on the funding and spending side, libraries can increase the resilience of their budget, allowing them to protect their core mission even in times of reduced funding.

THE ASSESSMENT TOOL—PART 4: LIBRARY BUDGETS

1. Diversifying Funding Sources

Consider your library's budget and what percentage of incoming funds come from what sources. How many different sources are represented? Does your library seek out grants and support staff seeking training opportunities for grant writing? For academic libraries, does your library have a relationship with the Development Office and work to keep the library on their agenda? What kind of marketing toward donors does the library do? Would a regular newsletter or a brochure detailing how to give to the library be a useful tool? What about the Friends of the Library group? Is there one and do they have a record of successful fundraising? Are there other options for additional funding that should be pursued?

Diversifying funding sources can be an important part of an overall budget control policy. By seeking support outside of our primary funders we both increase the health of our libraries and increase the range of what we can do and so serve our patrons better. It also benefits our funding institutions by increasing the value of the dollars they have given us and allowing them to go further. As part of your sustainability plan, consider increasing support for staff to learn how to write grant proposals and investigating expanding your marketing to potential donors. Also consider continuing education for administrators in fundraising. Additional coursework and workshops may be a worthwhile investment.

THE ASSESSMENT TOOL—PART 4: LIBRARY BUDGETS (continued)

2. Considering the Collection

Examine your collection spending in detail, especially journal and other periodical expenses. Does the way you are spending your collection budget meet your library's particular goals? How much of your budget is tied up in large packages, ones where only a small group of the subscribed titles are getting use? What percentage of your budget is tied up in multiyear contracts and how closely is usage scrutinized before contracts are negotiated when they expire? Are you using and promoting your state-funded suite of databases? Are there other areas of the collection where spending should be directed to better meet the needs of the library's patrons?

Controlling spending is an important step in increasing the sustainability of libraries, but libraries are spending institutions. We buy things; this is as fundamental a part of our mission as making those things available. Unfortunately, some companies have exploited this necessity and have used it to their advantage. The combination of the rise of the "big deal" and rapidly changing technology has combined to create incredible budget strain and led to a reduction in resources put toward traditional books and far greater investment in technological equipment and journals. The need for technology is, of course, perfectly legitimate and serves many communities very well, especially communities whose members do not have access to technology at home. The expansion of the collection though, while seeming quite nice on the surface, may not actually be supporting our patrons as much as we had hoped or publishers had promised.

Research on this area is still slim as the SUSHI protocol for usage statistics is still being implemented and many libraries have not yet had time to undertake comprehensive studies of their collections and none have yet published them. SUSHI stands for Standardized Usage Statistics Harvesting Initiative and is a computer protocol intended to allow for faster and simpler gathering of usage information from across vendor platforms. While information gathered using this protocol is still slim, previous work on incorporating usage statistics into collection development decisions indicates that libraries are paying an enormous amount of money for materials that are used very little or not at all.[4] For some libraries, providing access to this broad range of less used materials is part of their mission and a perfectly legitimate use of funds. Most libraries, however, are not research libraries and have at best a few areas of specialization in which they collect deeply. For those libraries, examining usage carefully is very important as part of being a good steward of the budget. Despite this fact, at this time, the process needed to get high-quality usage data is at best burdensome and at worse literally impossible. As the number of scholarly journal articles published each year has soared and libraries have signed on to big deals to ensure access to those articles, many of us have had hardly a clue about what we actually have access to at any given moment and what our patrons are actually using. Combine this with the incredible time commitment that would be required to actually stay on top of the ever-changing set of materials that we have access to through aggregators, and it becomes apparent that in many ways we have lost control of our collection and ceded that control to the publishing and database industry. Reclaiming this control by trudging through our data and then using that data to make wise decisions is an important step in building sustainable library collections.

TRANSFORMING THE INFORMATION ECOSYSTEM FROM WITHIN

Controlling our own collections is an important step in creating healthy budgets and strong collections, but it is also a stopgap solution to a problem that deserves collective action. Sustainability requires moving past temporary measures to long-term solutions that are resilient and meet the needs of all stakeholders. Building a new system for scholarly communication, one that allows the widest access possible to the scholarly record, is important if we want to see healthy libraries in the future. Collective action at the level of the profession is discussed in part three, but individual libraries also have a role to play in creating a new healthy system. Supporting or, if needed, leading open access initiatives, making wise licensing decisions, and working together through consortia and the traditional interlibrary loan system are good first steps libraries can take that can be done locally and according to local needs and interests, ones that will meet the needs not only of our local patrons, but also ones that will support the development of a stronger information ecosystem in general.

THE ASSESSMENT TOOL—PART 5: TRANSFORMING THE INFORMATION ECOSYSTEM FROM WITHIN

1. Open Access

What can the library do to make an open access initiative on your campus a viable idea? Is there a conversation happening now that the library can contribute to or should the library start that conversation? Is there funding available to bring in speakers or host a symposium on open access? What about an institutional repository? How could that fit into the existing set of supports the library and institution currently offer? How could it be funded and maintained?

The post-WWII era saw an incredible explosion in the number of journals published. This explosion was accompanied by a transition from small not-for-profit presses into the large consolidated market we see today.[5] That market benefits first from the unpaid labor of the scholars who create their products, mostly faculty members who operate in a gift economy and labor for tenure and other benefits that come not from publishers, but from their institutions and disciplines, and second from the limited ability of libraries to refuse overpriced materials. As this problem has grown over the years the idea of creating a new model, an open access model that keeps the published results of research within the gift economy, has developed and gained considerable strength. It is this model that has every chance and every hope of meeting the needs of scholars, students, and citizens going forward.

This model, however, cannot grow and thrive without our strong support. As the ones who mind the budgets and have the opportunity to see the system as a whole, librarians have a special role to play in supporting the transition. It is a new role and one that feels uncomfortable for many of us. After all, we are a service profession; telling our faculty that they need to change the way they publish is far outside our usual role. That explains why most libraries are still in the early stages of educating their faculty about open access issues and helping them as authors transition to an open access model. Some libraries are further along in the process, and a very few, Harvard, MIT, and Hope College among them, have completed it. Each campus will have a different path toward developing an open access policy for campus, but placing this as a high priority in your sustainability plan can help to direct adequate resources toward the project.

**THE ASSESSMENT TOOL—PART 5: TRANSFORMING THE
INFORMATION ECOSYSTEM FROM WITHIN** (continued)

2. Wise Licensing

Review your existing licenses for objectionable terms such as not allowing interlibrary loan, limiting access for in-building users, attempts to limit
the use of the resource for electronic reserves, attempts to preempt fair
use doctrine, and other overreaches. Consider how these licenses can be
renegotiated when they are up for renewal. Look at how much support for
staff development is available to support those engaged in negotiations
and consider whether it should be increased.

Back in the dark ages, before computers, the library subscribed to a journal, it came in the mail, eventually it was bound and it then lived forever-
more on the shelf as part of the library's collection. There is no doubt that the
advent of electronic journals and other aggregated databases is a far superior
method of providing access to scholarly literature. It is far more convenient,
far easier to search, allows full-text searching, and frees of us all from the pho-
tocopier. The problem is not with the technology, the problem is with the role
that corporations, especially the large multinational publishers, have played
in this new system. Given the long history of our profession, negotiating
license agreements is a relatively new skill that librarians have had to develop
in reaction to the change from an ownership model to an access model. Learning to read contracts, understand terms, and negotiate for improvements is
tricky, but there are excellent resources available to help you in the professional literature. Protecting the access and searchability that have made the
contemporary library such a pleasure to use, and protecting it for all users,
not simply those at wealthy institutions or in large cities, is a crucial part of
sustaining libraries over the long term and should be a part of most libraries'
sustainability plans.

**THE ASSESSMENT TOOL—PART 5: TRANSFORMING
THE INFORMATION ECOSYSTEM FROM WITHIN** (continued)

3. Strengthening Consortiums and Other Interlibrary Relationships

Review the library's existing consortial relationships and consider what
those relationships bring to library. Is the consortium working well or should
the library invest time and effort in improving their consortial relationships?
Are there other consortia active locally that would be a good fit? What
about interlibrary loan agreements? Is the library active in reciprocal relationships that would reduce borrowing cost and time while at the same time
contributing to the strength of the interlibrary loan system?

If a university or city administrator knows one thing about the funding of libraries, they know that participation in library consortia can save money. The evolution of library consortia from the early days of union catalogs and interlibrary lending agreements, through the development of bibliographic utilities and automation groups through to purchasing consortia, demonstrates a core strength of librarianship: cooperation and collective action. It would be hard to imagine the library world today without OCLC and its regional collectives, state-based groups like OhioLink, and smaller groups like the reciprocal interlibrary loan group Libraries Very Interested In Sharing. These groups allow us to do far more than our individual institutions could accomplish alone and they can serve as a model as we try and create new strategies that will allow us to move forward as resources become ever more constrained in the future.

Building on this legacy are the open source software projects like OLE and Evergreen that are working to reclaim the software we rely on most, the integrated library system (ILS). These projects, and others including those focused on building a strong searching and storage infrastructure for an open access publishing model, need and deserve our strong support. They need us to be willing to take risks and commit resources to make them work. By supporting these projects and groups as part of your library's sustainability plan you can institutionalize that support and contribute to building the library systems of the future, ones that we will badly need going forward.

SUPPORTING YOUR LOCAL ECONOMY

The economic sustainability of the library and information systems we depend on to provide services to our patrons is only one part of the larger sustainability mission of libraries. The other part, equally important for all types of libraries, is supporting and, in some cases, helping to rebuild the local economy of our communities. Most public libraries are already strong supporters of the local business community through their role as information providers. Strengthening this support and expanding it can be one component of a long-term strategy to enhance local economic development. Of course, libraries also have important roles as consumers, as employers, and as community leaders. Using these roles to support local business and the local community is an innovative way to contribute to building strong and resilient communities.

THE ASSESSMENT TOOL—PART 6:
SUPPORTING YOUR LOCAL ECONOMY

1. Participating in the Local Economy

Consider the non-materials purchases your library makes. Who are your primary vendors and are there local alternatives that could competitively supply some part of your regular purchases? Review your vendor lists and compare them with the locally owned businesses in your community. Review your web presence and the services you currently offer to local entrepreneurs. Is the collection supporting this group of patrons and are there improvements that could be made to enhance this part of the collection. What about programming? Are there targeted programs for this group, perhaps workshops on finding industry and company information or one on navigating local and state regulatory information?

A healthy local economy is the backbone for creating a strong and resilient society. Without it library resources dry up, local people suffer, and environmental concerns end up being sacrificed on the altar of job creation. Libraries are one of the most important resources in any community for leveling the playing field and supporting small businesses through the provision of information, information that would otherwise only be available to large companies, is a great way to both build support for the library and help the community.

Buying locally too is a great way to help the local economy. Ordering books through a local independent bookstore, getting basic office supplies from a local vendor, and employing service people like electricians and plumbers all contribute toward a healthier local economy. Libraries in suburban and rural areas especially can have a strong influence by keeping local dollars local. Looking for opportunities to do this and institutionalizing this goal as part of a sustainability plan make a strong statement about the library's support of the local business community.

NOTES

1. John Buschmann, *Dismantling the Public Sphere: Situating and Sustaining Librarianship in the Age of the New Public Philosophy* (Westport, CN: Libraries Unlimited, 2013).
2. Heather Morrison, "Freedom for Scholarship in the Internet Age" (PhD Diss., Simon Fraser University, 2012).
3. David Salt and B. H. Walker, *Resilience Thinking: Sustaining Ecosystems and People in a Changing World* (Washington, DC: Island Press, 2006), 1.

4. For an example, see Philip M. Davis, "Where to Spend Our E-journal Money? Defining a University Library's Core Collection Through Citation Analysis," *Portal: Libraries & the Academy* 2, no. 1 (January 2002): 155.

5. Jean-Claude Guédon, *In Oldenburg's Long Shadow: Librarians, Research Scientists, Publishers, and the Control of Scientific Publishing* (Washington, DC: Association of Research Libraries, 2001).

6
Equity

___

E quity seems an odd part of the largely practical and technologically focused philosophy of sustainability. While the environmental and economic aspects seem make sense intuitively, equity seems out of place, offering little in the way of immediate practical solutions. But, in fact, it is equity, the idea that justice, fairness, and a basic standard of living are shared rights due to all members of society, that underlies the entire philosophy. Equity, both intergenerational and intragenerational, serves as the unifying principle that holds the concept of sustainability together and allows it to form a coherent whole. The focus on intergenerational equity, that is, equity between generations, tells us that we have to create solutions and make decisions that will not harm future people, our children, grandchildren, and so on. Intragenerational equity tells us that we need also to be attentive to the people of today and ensure that we do not harm the current generation. Equity then is what keeps human flourishing at the center of sustainability and requires us to carefully consider how changes and decisions we make today will impact future generations, the poor, people from historically marginalized cultures, and everyone else.

To better understand the role that equity plays in the philosophy and practice of sustainability, consider an example from outside of the library, the idea of a carbon tax. A carbon tax could be implemented in a very progressive way, as suggested by James Hansen of NASA, by taxing fossil fuels at mines and wells for domestic sources and at the port of entry for imported oil and coal. The taxes gathered could then be returned to citizens in the form of a dividend, similar to the way Alaska manages its oil revenues. A carbon tax could also be levied at the point of purchase, or the money from a point of entry tax could be gathered and used for government spending in general. Both of the latter two options would help to reduce carbon pollution, but at the cost of the poor being priced out of the market or at least suffering a disproportionate impact. Equity is the sustainability value that guides the way we think about these issues. It is the value that causes us to stop and say, "Yes, we must reduce carbon pollution rapidly, but not at the cost of families going without heat or low income wage earners struggling to afford gasoline."

By keeping equity as a fundamental measurement of the success of sustainability efforts, the solutions to environmental and economic problems can be both sustainable, because solutions that are oppressive and exclude the needs of some people tend to create backlash and fail while also leading us toward the kind of world that allows libraries to flourish. This is why, in some ways, equity is the easiest of the three Es for libraries looking for a successful sustainability effort. As a value, equity requires us to create the kind of human relationships that make the world a kinder and more pleasant place to live, one based on democratic values and basic human decency. Both are goals that most libraries have implicitly embedded into their existing missions. This is not to say that libraries do not have quite a bit of work to do toward the goal of creating a more equitable society; there are many areas libraries can and should focus on improving as part of the transition to a more equitable library.

In general, equity work for libraries falls into three broad areas. The first is working with marginalized patrons. For many libraries this means improving service to linguistic minorities, poor and unemployed patrons, and ethnic and racial minority groups by developing strong collections and high-quality programming meant to serve these groups. The second area is within the library itself. By becoming a better employer, especially to paraprofessionals and clerks, libraries can increase the well-being of their communities while improving their own organizations. The third area for most libraries involves the changes we can make internally in our collection decisions to support the political work of reforming fair use, evolving the right of first sale, and protecting patron privacy. While it may seem unusual to pull these disparate activities together, they are actually linked very closely—through the value of equity.

THE ASSESSMENT TOOL—PART 7.1:
MEETING THE NEEDS OF THE LOCAL COMMUNITY

1. Serving Marginalized Community Members

Which marginalized groups within your community does the library currently seek to serve through collections and programming? Review the census data for your community or the demographics for your university. Are there specific racial and ethnic groups who are represented in the community, but not in your collections or programming? Does the collection reflect the linguistic makeup of the community, offering at least something for each group to read in their native language? What about economic groups? Is the library making an effort to meet the needs of working class and poor patrons in proportion to their representation in the community? Is there programming aimed at the interests and concerns of working class and poor members of the community? Review the literacy rate of the local community using either the National Assessment of Adult Literacy or other dataset and consider whether the library should be more active in supporting and developing adult literacy programs. Look at the library's existing advisory groups. Is the membership diverse or should there be a special recruitment effort to build diversity? Finally, are there local or campus based groups that the library should join to learn how to better support minority and poor patrons and to offer that support to those already involved in targeted programming?

This item has greater relevance for public libraries, but academic libraries, even those with curriculum centered collections, should also carefully consider the questions. Most campuses struggle in some way with supporting students from minority backgrounds and all schools struggle with adequately supporting the needs of students from poor families. Developing collections and programming meant to serve these groups is challenging but important. There are excellent resources listed in appendix C for developing non-English collections and for improving programming aimed at minority and poor patrons. This also represents a good opportunity for outreach to community and campus groups who work to improve the well-being of these groups. For example, many campuses have groups like Campus Alliance of La Raza or traditionally black Greek organizations who would be excellent partners in helping to build collections or design programming. Most communities also have adult literacy groups who could advise and assist the library in reaching out to low literacy adults. These groups could also help the library recruit a more diverse membership for its advisory boards, if that is needed.

THE ASSESSMENT TOOL—PART 7.1:
MEETING THE NEEDS OF THE LOCAL COMMUNITY (continued)

2. The Library as an Employer

Consider the library as whole and, if possible, review the pay scales. Are they reasonable and do they meet the living wage requirements of your area? Does the library pay those lowest on the scale enough to actually live in the area? Is the difference between the highest paid employee and the lowest paid employee greater than 20?[1] Does the library create part-time jobs to avoid paying benefits or because the job makes the most sense as a part-time position? What about the library's leave policies? Are they equitable and reasonable? Consider family and sick leave carefully; would the library benefit from a more generous policy, one that allows sick employees to stay out of the workplace or care for ill family members? Beyond compensation issues, consider workplace democracy. Is there a forum for all library employees to have their voices heard? Is the relationship between the library administration and the union, if there is one, good? If not, what could be done to improve it?

Not every library is in a position to even evaluate these issues, especially the ones involving compensation and benefits. If this section is not likely to help your library sustainability efforts, do skip it. These are tricky issues and ones that many libraries do not have the ability to control. However, there are some aspects of equitable employment that libraries can control and that can be implemented with little or no budget impact. Issues of voice in the workplace are a key example of this. Creating a workers council or other forum to allow employees to discuss issues important to them is a good step in developing a more equitable workplace. By allowing workers, especially paraprofessionals and clerks, the opportunity to both contribute to decision making and bring forth ideas of their own, workers gain more control over their work and a greater sense of being respected. The same could be said of modifying leave policies by creating time sharing schemes for workers with the need for more leave than is typically granted. By allowing workers to share leave time, all workers can be confident that they will not face loss of pay or their jobs because of illness.

THE ASSESSMENT TOOL—PART 7.2:
PROTECTING THE RIGHT TO READ

1. Protecting Fair Use

Is your staff well trained and do they understand both the statutory and case law surrounding fair use? Are they able to communicate that information effectively to patrons when needed? For academic libraries, how do the policies governing your reserve desk and electronic reserves align with the current best practices as laid out in the Code of Best Practices for Fair Use in Academic and Research Libraries? Are your policies reasonably risk tolerant, especially in light of the recent Georgia State win? What about your license agreements? Are you involved in licenses that severely restrict your patrons' fair use rights and, if so, can they be renegotiated?

As a librarian with responsibility for a large and popular reserve collection, few issues are closer to my heart than the need to preserve fair use. The greyness and uncertainty that have hung over reserve desks and other digitization projects now seems to be in the process of lifting. With the recent win in Georgia and the publication of the *Code of Best Practices in Fair Use for Academic and Research Libraries* we have strong updated guidance, both from the courts and from the profession.[2] With this information in hand, we can now turn to revising our own policies and creating ones that work for the way our patrons need to use our materials. Incorporating this as a sustainability activity helps to situate and contextualize the work into a larger framework—namely the need to build libraries that can sustain their budgets over the long term and do not simply act as a money funnel to large publishers.

License agreements are also an area to examine closely. Some publishers will attempt to restrict fair use rights in their licenses. Fighting against this will help to strengthen and protect fair use rights. It will also ease educating your patrons about reasonable boundaries, by ensuring that the boundaries are reasonable and as uniform as possible across products.

THE ASSESSMENT TOOL—PART 7.2:
PROTECTING THE RIGHT TO READ (continued)

2. Evolving the Right of First Sale for the Digital Environment

Are library staff well educated about the legal complexities involved in the lending of e-books? Are they familiar with the various alternate models and do they have the tools and the time to follow news and legal cases as they evolve? Has the library articulated a set of goals for what it wants in an e-book package and presented these goals to publishers as part of the negotiation process?

The rise of the e-book is possibly the most disruptive technology yet for librarians. Its very nature renders moot the most important legal protection that libraries have had—the right of first sale. The right of first sale, the right to lend, resell, or otherwise dispose of one's own property, is the legal basis of the entire lending library. Without it we are left standing, rather unsteadily, on tradition and the idea that libraries perform an important role in society. On a practical level, without it we are left at the mercy of often fickle publishers and their lawyers. Since the nature of digital books precludes the right of first sale, because each use essentially creates a new copy, we need to advocate forcefully for a new model for born digital materials, one that allows us to continue to lend and still allows publishers and authors some reasonable measure of profit. Working with publishers and advocating forcefully in our own negotiations for a reasonable lending scheme for e-books, one that allows as many checkouts as we could reasonably expect from a print book, one that allows us to lend materials through interlibrary loan, and one that ensures our patrons' privacy is protected is a crucial part of building a sustainable model for the 21st century.

THE ASSESSMENT TOOL—PART 7.2:
PROTECTING THE RIGHT TO READ (continued)

3. Guarding Patron Privacy

Look at your library's privacy and confidentiality policies and consider whether your license agreements with vendors, including any hosted software systems, comply with that policy. If you have hosted or cloud based systems is everyone who needs to be familiar with how they handle subpoenas and warrants? Do your state laws protect privacy and if so what happens when your data are hosted in another state or even another country? Consider creating a document listing your privacy priorities and the language in vendor contracts that support or fail to support those priorities. Use that as a starting point when renegotiating contracts and when choosing new vendors.

Edward Snowden's leak of classified information about the NSA's abilities to gather and search for private communication is only the latest in an ongoing series of revelations about the ability of the United States government to conduct surveillance on a mass scale against both foreign and US individuals. Combine this with the long history of direct government intrusion into patron privacy and the rise of cloud computing and the stage is set for massive violations of privacy on a scale never before dreamed of. As more and more libraries sign up for so-called NextGen library systems we are, collectively, handing over control of the records of millions and millions of library patrons to companies who are not bound by our professional ethics, do not share our values, and are not even always able to inform us of government inquiries. And that's without even opening the issue of corporate surveillance and what companies might be able to mine with the massive amounts of our patron data they currently possess.

The long-term systemic solution to this problem lays in the open source software solutions being built by libraries themselves. Those packages offer libraries a much higher level of control over both the code and the actual data. Implementing them can be more challenging, especially for smaller libraries with less in-house systems expertise, but doing so offers a real step in the fight against the constant erosion of privacy both within libraries and the larger society. Early in my career, I remember being informed by a librarian friend and techno-enthusiast that concerns about privacy were quaint and "only librarians care about privacy." Those days are gone. Patrons care very much about their privacy and have a much better understanding of why it is important to preserve it. And when they do not, part of our role is to educate them. Protecting the privacy of our patrons is now more important than ever. It is also far harder than ever and almost certainly requires an ever increasing level commitment and technical skill. Including patron privacy preservation in your sustainability plan is an important step toward creating the library of our future—a future that embraces one of our longest standing and most closely held values at its center.

NOTES

1. For a discussion on the CEO/worker pay ratio, see Gary Shorter, "The Pay Ratio Provision," in *Dodd-Frank Act: Legislation to Repeal It in the 113th Congress* (Washington, DC: Library of Congress, Congressional Research Service, October 28, 2013).
2. Prudence S. Adler, Patricia Aufderheide, Brandon Butler, Peter Jaszi, *Code of Best Practices in Fair Use for Academic and Research Libraries* (Washington, DC: Association of Research Libraries, January 2012).

PART III

Sustainable Librarianship in Practice

7
The Challenges of Technology and Corporate Power in the Library

Creating a sustainability plan for your library is important. Without changes at the library level, we cannot have changes at the level of the information system as whole. To build a whole new kind of library system though, we need to confront the problems in the information system directly, as an organized profession. Without confronting power directly, we cannot be successful. It is the difference between recycling and the passing of the Clean Water Act. Recycling is popular in large part because it threatens no one while creating an industry of its own—one with a powerful constituency of corporate actors who can advocate for themselves and encourage citizens to use their services. No one loses out; there is no shortage of garbage causing landfill companies to go out business. Instead, it can be a win-win situation. Like with most of the library sustainability efforts suggested in previous chapters, recycling makes people feel good, makes other people money, and creates very little resistance among those who currently hold power because it threatens no one. Passing and enforcing the Clean Water Act, in contrast, was and is far more challenging. It costs a considerable amount of money both for taxpayers and for companies. It is constantly being questioned, ignored, and fought directly by those whose behavior it restricts, while very few people visit their local waterway and think, "Wow this would be even more polluted if not for the Clean Water Act!" And yet, it is the Clean Water Act and not recycling that has arguably been the larger benefit to the environment over the past 30 years. A library sustainability plan is like recycling. We should all do it, it is important, but it will never lead to the kind of changes needed on its own. For that, we need a Clean Water Act. The library equivalent of the Clean Water Act is what the next two chapters describe. But before we can get there, we need to lay out clearly why we need change and what needs to change.

THE ACTUALIZATION OF THE DIGITAL LIBRARY

The great library educator and philosopher Jesse Shera once wrote, "We could have in this whole new information science something as potentially dangerous as the atomic bomb."[1] Likely, he had no idea how very true his words were, though not in the way he expected. His claim hinged on the idea that expansive changes in technology—the computer, the microform, and various other gadgets—required the profession to transform itself so that new technologies could be used well and controlled by those who had the best interest of the public at heart. Part of that, in his view, was keeping them in the right hands, with those who would not use these new technologies for "antisocial" purposes. As he wrote, "We simply have to establish safeguards, social and political safeguards so that these mechanical advances are used for the proper ends, and so not fall into the wrong hands, that they are not misused."[2] From the perspective of the 21st century, his comments seem both quaint and antiquated. The idea that it might be possible to keep a technology out of the wrong hands and so ensure that it is used for prosocial purposes is no longer reasonable; we have decades of experience and billions of dollars wasted in pointless wars that underscore that fact. Whether it is keeping nuclear weapons away from countries the United States believes dangerous or keeping Google in hands that live up to the motto "don't be evil," time has shown that once a technology exists it will be used badly, for corporate gain or for national power, by those who seek to turn it into a weapon of war or commerce.

Jesse Shera lived through an era—his professional career spanned the 1930s through the 1970s—that was perhaps even more subject to life-altering change than our own, including the almost universal adoption of the automobile, universal access to electricity, to the beginnings of what we now call the information revolution. His was an era of justified optimism peppered with strong social movements that improved life for the far better for most Americans. As far back as 1967 he pointed out, "For generations, the scholar has dreamed of a utopia in which he would have access to the total store of materials and the ability to choose from it only the best documents for his immediate need."[3] We now live in a version of that utopia, or at least some of us do. The technical challenges of the so-called "library problem" have been solved by and large, and solved well. There is no technological reason that almost everybody in the United States cannot walk into their local public library, locate, and retrieve, or request via interlibrary loan, almost any document or book they wish to read. And there is no technological reason that anyone with access to the internet cannot use a search engine and gain access to the wide bulk of medical, scholarly, and scientific literature. The problem, which Shera hints at in his writings but never confronts directly, is that within our society technology is always the tool of the powerful, and the more powerful the technology, the truer this is. And the more libraries rely on that technology to do our daily work and fulfill our missions, the more vulnerable we have become to those in power.

It is here, at the intersection of power and technology within the library that we find the greatest challenge to contemporary librarianship. It did not have to be this way. In 1998, Jean-Claude Guédon outlined what he called the "virtual library."[4] Guédon's virtual library was a utopian vision, and a warning. The ongoing increases in the price of journals, the massive transition to electronic publishing, and the transformation of the scholarly journal economy into a market economy were well under way. Guédon warned, "Libraries remain our very best hope to prevent basic human knowledge from being completely privatized, monopolized, and ultimately locked up by venal interests. Librarians must never forget that point and scholars should quickly come to assist as they recognize that librarians are their best ramparts against a commercial ethos that may undermine their intellectual and individual integrity."[5] Guédon's vision for the future was one where libraries had built the safeguards that Shera called for; it was one where libraries made the transition from collectors to publishers, one where libraries had taken a central role in the production and dissemination of knowledge itself. It was a vision where the knowledge bounty that technology allows was used to the benefit of all, instead of locked behind digital walls and converted into a commodity for profit.

From the perspective of 15 years later it is easy to see the open access movement as the direct descendant of this vision. But it is also easy to see that between attempts to co-opt the movement by publishers and the struggles libraries have with advocating for a new system, we have largely failed as a profession in realizing Guédon's vision. While we have dithered and discussed new models, new ways of actualizing the potential of digital libraries, corporate interests have not. The actualization of the digital library has taken on a particular form, one that presents considerable danger to libraries and our readers. We have allowed commercial interests to claim "ownership" of the scholarly record through digitization and publishing. In doing so we have allowed an unhealthy system to grow. This system leads to libraries that have been hollowed out, reduced to access points with librarians as skilled product trainers, while the publishers themselves profit handsomely from the labor of the very scholars we support and from the citizens whose taxes support us all. It has led to a system where a scholarly article, one researched and written on the taxpayer and nonprofit dime, can be purchased on the web for $35 and hardly anyone seems to be angry enough to object beyond strongly written statements. That we have allowed this to happen is not surprising. Corporate interests have taken considerable power throughout the economy since the 1980s. But, as they say, another world is possible. What is does not have to be and by exploring the failure of the current system we can begin to see a path to a new information system. One rooted firmly in library values, serving us, our readers, and the larger world in which we all live. And most importantly, one that can withstand the challenges we are facing in the 21st century while making widely available the legacy of human knowledge that it is our profession's duty to preserve and share.

It is important to distinguish here between the fact of digitized information, specifically the rather glorious product that is the contemporary database, and the political economy that this product has fostered. Or to quote Shera again, "Now, lest we be misunderstood, we want to emphasize . . . that we yield to no one in our enthusiasm for the computer and what its obvious power can bring to the library."[6] It warrants saying again that though the Luddites, both contemporary and historical, all have my most sincere sympathies and solidarity in their fight, I am not against technology nor am I advocating for a return to the long lost days of card catalogs and bound journals. Instead, like the original Luddites who were objecting not to the machines themselves, but rather to the changes in the economy that they fostered, so I am critiquing the political economy of knowledge. That economy has been enabled by technology and has developed simultaneously with the rather incredible advances of that technology, but it is distinct from it. What I am critiquing is the state of being that Estabrook predicted in response to Daniel Bell's optimistic prediction that power in society would transition from the owners of capital to those who could control information. Estabrook's rebuttal to Bell's prediction, "It does not necessarily follow . . . that the ownership of capital will be replaced by the ownership of knowledge as the basis for societal power. Rather, it can be argued that, as information becomes more important, the owners of capital will appropriate the information utilities more directly for their purposes."[7] The problems that have arisen since Estabrook's prediction in 1981, detailed below, are not inherent to computer based storage and retrieval of information, but are rather caused by the particular place, time, and social milieu in which the technology developed. It could have been otherwise and it can be otherwise.

THE DIGITAL LIBRARY AND THE ENCLOSURE
OF THE INFORMATION ECOSYSTEM

The consolidation of the publishing industry into a few behemoths and the all encompassing nature of a webscale ILS surely would have taken Shera and his contemporaries by surprise. I suspect even Guédon is startled by the sheer scale of the current system. Librarians in Shera's day did not foresee the extent to which the advent of high technology and its application to the "library problem" would lead to the old process of enclosure. Hence, a technological problem has been replaced with an economic problem with the result that the full utopia once imagined cannot come into being.

Enclosure is the process of taking a previously shared resource, a grazing field, a water source, or even information, and erecting barriers to use. The most well-known example of an enclosure movement is in the sheep grazing common of England in the Middle Ages. There first the nobles, and then eventually those who had been made wealthy through industrialization, began taking land that had previously been used by all members of a village for their own private use. The goal was to raise as many sheep as possible for the new mills being built in the cities. As a contemporary poem describes the process:

> The law locks up the man or woman
> Who steals the goose from off the common
> But leaves the greater villain loose
> Who steals the common from off the goose.
>
> The law demands that we atone
> When we take things we do not own
> But leaves the lords and ladies fine
> Who take things that are yours and mine.
>
> The poor and wretched don't escape
> If they conspire the law to break;
> This must be so but they endure
> Those who conspire to make the law.
>
> The law locks up the man or woman
> Who steals the goose from off the common
> And geese will still a common lack
> Till they go and steal it back.
>
> Anonymous[8]

The result of this process, whose utter brutality should not be overlooked, was indeed more wool and also the creation of the first urban industrial working class. As Karl Polanyi says in *The Great Transformation*, "Enclosures have appropriately been called a revolution of the rich against the poor."[9] The current enclosure movement is no different.

But how do we move from the agricultural and budding industrial economy of England to the contemporary information economy? Vandana Shiva, in her book *Earth Democracy*, lays out a five-step process for enclosing a common, one that can be seen at work in the information economy as much as in the sheep grazing fields of old England.[10] The first step she identifies is, "the exclusion of people from resources that had been their common property or held in common." This process can be seen in biotechnology patents that allow seeds from particular plants to be turned into intellectual property so that they cannot be used without payment to their "owners," in the patenting of biological processes, and in the continual extension of copyright terms at the expense of the public domain. From a library perspective, we can see this process most clearly in the scholarly journal economy. These articles are written for tenure, for prestige, to communicate an important advance and then they are then handed over to commercial publishers for distribution, largely back to libraries. The problem is that with the advent of digital technology and the internet publishers have chosen to charge enormous amounts of money to access these articles, thereby putting up digital fences and excluding a large part of the potential readership.

This leads to Shiva's second step, "the creation of 'surplus' or 'disposable' people . . . ." These people, whom we see today most acutely in the unemployed scholar, the recent graduate, those not covered by a large and well-funded public library system, and most of all in the people of the global South, are now in a position of being denied access, not because of a lack of ability on our part to bring them the materials they need, but to preserve the profit of publishers and database companies. These are our 'disposable' people. A technological barrier has been replaced with an economic barrier. And like the landless peasants of England who starved among plenty, so too do our disposable people suffer. Lack of access to medical information for doctors, nurses, and other medical professionals is one serious consequence. They, along with their patients, qualify as "disposable" under our current information system. Consider the case of medical professionals in parts of Africa. In a descriptive study of the use of medical literature by postgraduate doctors and medical researchers by Smith et al., "Respondents frequently described locating an article of interest only to find that it needs a subscription." They reported problems accessing articles for free even within so-called "free initiatives"; for example, "HINARI has a common password for this institution, but users are discouraged because they say at times some cost must be incurred if full text is requested."[11]

Thirdly, Shiva identifies "the creating of private property by the enclosure of common property." Continuing to examine the case of scholarly journals, in the pre-digital days a journal became part of the larger common that is a library collection. And the combined physical collections of the libraries of the United States have long been a genuine common built from the smaller common of individual libraries' collections. From the early days of the National Catalog, interlibrary loan has been a thriving and important service offered by libraries. Union catalogs, and later services like RLN and OCLC, attest to the work the profession put into creating a system that could be shared broadly. The material was still covered under copyright, but the ability to read the item faced only the inherent restriction of physicality and the readers' intellectual limits. It is easy to see though why earlier librarians were so eager to see at least the first restriction lifted. Physical items are inferior in many ways to digital items. With the proliferation of smart phones and e-readers, the wealth of human knowledge could realistically be made available to anyone with access to the Internet and a high level of literacy. There will likely always be the so-called "long tail," but most of what people want to read and want to know could easily be made available. It is the transformation of that knowledge into private property, into an almost eternal source of profit for a small group of publishers, that has stood in the way. We can see this see in the idea that libraries should pay an ongoing, eternal toll for access to information that was previously owned outright, a toll far in excess of what it costs to maintain the servers and networks that support that access.

The next step in the enclosure process Shiva lays out is "the replacement of diversity that provides for multiple needs and performs functions with monocultures that provide raw materials for the market." *In Oldenburg's Long Shadow*, a history of scholarly publishing by Guédon, we see a strong proliferation of a wide variety of scholarly publishers in the early part of the last century.[12] We see each learned society supporting its members with the publication of journals, we see some commercial participation, and we see most of all that the many disciplines and subdisciplines each had their own set of journals, published by a multiplicity of sources. Guédon cites the *Science Citation Index* as a key player in the identification of potentially valuable titles and the precipitating factor that led to the flood of commercial interest in scholarly publishing. Whether he is correct or not in his analysis of the cause, currently 42 percent of academic journals are controlled by three massive publishers.[13] The diversity the scholarly publishing system previously benefited from has vanished, to be replaced by a few large multinational corporations reaping profits off the backs of an ever growing number of scholars and an ever shrinking pool of library resources.

Fifth, "The enclosure of minds and imagination with the result that enclosures are defined and perceived as universal human progress, not as growth of privilege and exclusive rights for a few and the dispossession and impoverishment for the many." The large commercial publishers and library product vendors would have us believe that their outsized profits are due to them for their beneficence in creating the products we all rely on, for building the database and the integrated library system. They would also have us believe that the current system is the only one possible, that large commercial enterprises are the only method of providing access to digital information, despite the access challenges they present. They discourage us from thinking seriously about what a different system could look like, what other choices we could make as a profession to ensure that we fulfill our mission of universal access while not bankrupting ourselves. Alongside this effort, they are working their best to co-opt the open access movement and manipulate it for their benefit.[14] They are successful in this because we allow them to be. When we speak in hushed tones when criticizing vendors, when we sign agreements that keep how much we pay for a product secret, when we allow ourselves to be silenced in our criticism because it feels unseemly, we are complicit in their attempts to stifle our creativity and willingness to fight for our patrons.

THE ENCLOSED DIGITAL LIBRARY AND THE INDIVIDUAL LIBRARY

The impact that this perverse information system has on individual libraries is profound. From a larger perspective the system is one manifestation of the ongoing attempts to defund the public sector to the benefit of the commercial sector, similar to attempts to promote charter schools over public schools and high stakes tests provided by corporations who market curriculums to match. The impact of this program on libraries has been a hollowing out of our basic functions as we are converted into a conduit to send money to large corporations on the one hand and to send patrons to their products on the other. The term for this, first coined by Schiller in his work on the commercialization of culture, *Culture, Inc.* is library bypass strategies.[15] In 1989, when Schiller was writing, he envisioned products being sold directly to consumers. This is certainly a strategy still in evidence today. As a strategy though, it has one major fault: most people simply cannot afford to pay what information providers would like them to pay. Libraries themselves still offer a tempting target, with their large pools of money devoted to the purchase of information resources. More recently, the term has appeared in the library blogosphere in reference to e-books.[16] The argument again is that publishers will go around libraries and market their offerings directly to patrons. However, as Carl Grant argues, library bypass strategies can be much more subtle.[17] Considering the unlikelihood of any information corporation ignoring the temptations that library budgets represent, library bypass strategies were unlikely ever to be so straightforward. Instead of companies solely marketing to our patrons, what we see are libraries being bypassed in the selection of information resources themselves. We see this in the aggregated database, but also in large collections of e-books and discovery layers. Rather than the previous system, where we maintained a high degree of control over what was offered to our patrons, now much of that work has been handed over to the companies who provide the content, often via the discovery layer, which we will return to again shortly.

It is important to acknowledge that some of the problems in the contemporary library system are not caused by corporate control themselves, especially the problem of information overload. The dramatic increase in the number of published articles, journals, and books since the 1990s has only accelerated in recent years.[18] While the desire on the part of corporations to tap new markets is certainly part of the cause of this explosion, the ease of electronic publishing, the increase in the number and size of universities, and the "publish or perish" dictum have all contributed as well. Maintaining bibliographic control and developing collections in this environment was always going to be a challenge. For some, the solution to the metadata problem has been to argue for the curtailment of traditional metadata and its replacement with Google and Google-like interfaces. The Calhoun Report, for example, advocated a variety of simplifications to metadata urging, "Abandon the attempt to do comprehensive subject analysis manually with LCSH in favor of subject keywords; urge [Library of Congress] to dismantle LCSH."[19] You can see this same argument in OCLC's 2003 Environmental Scan report for libraries as well. That report proclaims, "Librarians and information professionals have had ample evidence for years that most searchers use a single term when searching—regardless of the sophistication of the interface. Why, then, do most library content interfaces still contain multiple search boxes?"[20] The report also lists unattributed quotes from "people OCLC interviewed" including this telling one, "Creation of copy cataloging is not a sustainable model—there is less and less need for human-generated cataloging and less ability to pay for it."[21] However, as David Bade effectively argues, "The arguments for all these practices have been the same: doing something takes more time than not doing something; therefore, let us not do something so we can save time (and money), timeliness being to sole criteria of quality. What is diminished in every case is access, and it is the user who suffers the increased cost in time and money."[22] This relinquishing of bibliographic control in favor of speedy and cheap cataloging is an abdication of our most basic duty, "to save the time of the reader."[23]

In addition to the loss of control, bibliographic and otherwise, the current information system creates a situation where the budget must grow every year just to keep pace and maintain the current collection. Unlike in the print days, keeping a steady budget means losing access not only to materials being published in the current year, but also to materials from past years. Not only that, but multiyear contracts keep us reliant on our existing products and leave little flexibility to change to new providers or select our resources more judiciously. It also means paying ongoing access fees for material we think we own. This loss of financial control combines with the loss of collection control to create a toxic situation that leaves libraries vulnerable to publishers and database vendors in ways not seen in the past. The drive to reduce costs feeds into the existing drive to outsource, eliminate skilled human cataloging, and give up our profession's previous commitment to our role as collection builders and organizers. The consequence of this is that we have allowed our collections to become black boxes whose contents and costs we can never be sure of. Quick! What percentage of PsycInfo is indexed in your discovery layer? What percentage of Sage Journals are indexed, and on what schedule is new metadata added? Who created that metadata and with what kind of user in mind? What about the *New York Times*? Do these seem absurd questions in the current information environment? Or do they seem like the kind of basic knowledge about a collection most reference librarians at least should readily know?

The discovery layer itself is the ultimate manifestation of this loss of control. Consider the decision by EBSCO to pull their metadata out of Primo, Ex Libris's discovery layer.[24] From a corporate strategy perspective it makes perfect sense not to support a competing product, but to the libraries left in the middle, especially those with numerous EBSCO products and Primo, it highlighted how little power libraries have in this economy. Our contracts and sunk investment costs lock us into these products, while companies maintain the right to change them without our consent. With no ability to influence what content we are providing and how that content is prioritized in the discovery layer, and in many cases not even firm answers to these questions, how can we say we are living up to our values and supporting our patrons well? When we are forbidden by nondisclosure agreements to even share with our own patrons what material is indexed in these products, how can we claim to be acting as good stewards of the collection? Products like this damage us as a profession and reveal just how vulnerable libraries have become to corporate machinations. More than that, it damages our relationship with our patrons and frustrates our efforts to support them. To quote Grant, "[Libraries] are selecting discovery tools that provide quick, pre-defined, pre-packaged content with a discovery interface that doesn't really meet the deeper needs of their users or their profession. Once they've done this, they've reduced their library's value-add in the information delivery chain and they've lost another valuable reason for maintaining their library's relevance within the institution and handed it to those that believe good enough is, well, good enough."[25] The discovery layer, perhaps more than any other recent development in the library world, highlights the fundamental power imbalance that exists in the information system as a whole. No single library is in a position to change this system alone. We need the profession as a whole to do that.

THE ENCLOSED DIGITAL LIBRARY AND THE LIBRARIAN

Librarians as professionals suffer too under the current system. By handing over so many of our fundamental tasks to vendors, collection development and cataloging for example, we have disempowered ourselves and reduced, as Carl Grant would say, our "value-add." But more than that, in doing so our role in our communities is reduced and our relationship with our patrons is betrayed. We cease to be a neutral and objective partner in the information search and retrieval process and instead become drawn into the role of marketer for our library's chosen set of products, always afraid that we are going to lose our jobs and even the entire profession to Internet search engines. As a profession, we have a rather serious problem, along with the other traditionally female professions, of self-doubt and criticism.[26] This history of doubting ourselves, our skills, and our importance inhibits us from organizing both within our individual institutions and as a profession. It inhibits us from pushing back hard when vendors feed us marketing speak and insist that privacy is only a concern of librarians. It inhibits us from fighting back when administrators push us to accept products we all know are inferior and confusing to our users. Writing in 1982, Wilson argued that librarians consider themselves a "minority group" and handle their identity as such.[27] I see little evidence that this has changed in the years since. Because we tend to see ourselves as a minority group and so seek not to identify with each other and with the profession as a whole, we are left vulnerable and divided, with serious consequences for ourselves and for the information system.

More than all of that, though, the system as it exists shelters us from the true consequences of our collective actions. We are protected from knowing the scale of the server farms and their carbon footprint. We do not have to worry about the proper disposal of outdated equipment. We are many steps removed from the mines where the ores and minerals that represent the physical manifestation of our digital collections were dug. The workers who built our equipment and those who maintain it never even receive a second thought from most of us. We live in a blissful ignorance that insulates us from the physical and social reality of our information system. And at the end of the day, that might be the largest problem we have. How can we advocate for change when we do not even realize we need change? How can we recognize ourselves as complicit in systems of destruction if we are never permitted to see that destruction? It is all too easy to claim that these concerns are too big, too broad, and too distant to deserve our attention, but if not us, if not one of the largest group of common keepers our society has, then who? Our organizations are morally accountable for the system we have allowed to prosper and into which we feed billions of dollars a year. If we are not responsible for its actions, than how can anyone be responsible for anything?

NOTES

1. Jesse Hauk Shera, *Sociological Foundations of Librarianship* (New York: Asia Pub. House, 1970), G81.
2. Ibid., G82.
3. J. H. Shera, "Librarians against Machines. Librarians Are Having Difficulty Adopting the New Technology Because They Have No Professional Philosophy," *Science* 156, no. 3776 (1967): 747.
4. Jean-Claude Guédon, "The Digital Library: An Oxymoron?" *Bulletin of the Medical Library Association* 87 (1999).
5. Ibid., 18.
6. Jesse Hauk Shera, *The Silent Stir of Thought: Or, What the Computer Cannot Do,* (Geneseo, NY: The College, 1969), 11.
7. Leigh Estabrook, "Productivity, Profit, and Libraries," *Library Journal* 106, no. 13 (1981): 1377.
8. Credit for plucking this poem out of obscurity goes to James Boyle, "The Second Enclosure Movement and the Construction of the Public Domain," *Law and Contemporary Problems* 66, no. 1/2 (2003).
9. Karl Polanyi, *The Great Transformation: The Political and Economic Origins of Our Time* (Boston: Beacon Press, 2001), 35.
10. Vandana Shiva, *Earth Democracy: Justice, Sustainability, and Peace* (Cambridge, MA: South End Press, 2005), 12.
11. Smith et al., "Access to Electronic Health Knowledge in Five Countries in Africa: A Descriptive Study," *BMC Health Services Research* 7 (2007).
12. Jean-Claude Guédon, *In Oldenburg's Long Shadow: Librarians, Research Scientists, Publishers, and the Control of Scientific Publishing* (Washington, DC: Association of Research Libraries, 2001).
13. Glenn S. McGuigan and Robert D. Russell, "The Business of Academic Publishing: A Strategic Analysis of the Academic Journal Publishing Industry and Its Impact on the Future of Scholarly Publishing," *Electronic Journal of Academic and Special Librarianship* 9, no. 3 (2008). http://southernlibrarianship.icaap.org/content/v09n03/mcguigan_g01.html.
14. Joseph J. Esposito, "Open Access 2.0: Access to Scholarly Publications Moves to a New Phase," *Journal of Electronic Publishing* 11, no. 2 (2008).
15. Herbert I. Schiller, *Culture, Inc.: The Corporate Takeover of Public Expression* (New York: Oxford University Press, 1989), 81.

16. Jean Costello, "Library Bypass Strategies," in *The Radical Patron: Extreme Thoughts on Public Libraries* (2009), www.radicalpatron.com/library-bypass-strategies.

17. Carl Grant, "Another Facet of the 'Library Bypass Strategies,'" *Thoughts from Carl Grant* (blog), November 16, 2009, http://thoughts.care-affiliates.com/2009/11/another-facet-of-library-bypass.html.

18. Andrew Odlyzko, "Open Access, Library and Publisher Competition, and the Evolution of General Commerce," Preprint. Submitted February 5, 2013, http://arxiv.org/abs/1302.1105.

19. Karen Calhoun, *The Changing Nature of the Catalog and Its Integration with Other Discovery Tools, Special report prepared at the request of the Library of Congress,* March 17, 2006, 18.

20. Cathy De Rosa, Lorcan Dempsey, and Alane Wilson, *The 2003 OCLC Environmental Scan: Pattern Recognition* (Dublin, OH: OCLC, 2003), 99.

21. Ibid., 79.

22. David W. Bade, *Responsible Librarianship: Library Policies for Unreliable Systems* (Duluth, MN: Library Juice Press, 2007), 48.

23. S. R. Ranganathan, *The Five Laws of Library Science*, Madras Library Association. Publication Series.2 (Madras, London: Madras Library Association; E. Goldston, 1931), 336.

24. Iris Jastram, "Heads They Win, Tails We Lose: Discovery Tools Will Never Deliver on Their Promise," *Pegasus Librarian* (blog), http://pegasuslibrarian.com/2011/01/heads-they-win-tales-we-lose-discovery-tools-will-never-deliver-on-their-promise.html, n2.

25. Grant, "Another Facet of the 'Library Bypass Strategies.'"

26. Roma M. Harris, *Librarianship: The Erosion of a Woman's Profession* (Norwood, NJ: Ablex, 1992), 61–76.

27. Pauline Wilson, *Stereotype and Status: Librarians in the United States*, Contributions in Librarianship and Information Science, no. 41 (Westport, CN: Greenwood Press, 1982), 138.

8
Curbing Corporate Power

The relationship between large corporations and libraries is, like the relationship between large corporations and practically all other institutions, one of fundamental power imbalance. Monopoly power, more properly called oligopoly power in the current setting, the kind we see in companies like Elsevier, McGraw-Hill, and, of course, Amazon is profoundly dangerous to the information system. Examples of the abuse of power abound. From unfair bundling practices, to ever rising prices, to cartel-like price setting, it is apparent that the power that these giant corporations are able to exert hurts libraries and the information system as a whole. Add in the power that these companies have to turn their economic power into political power through "donations" and lobbying, and it is quite plain that, if we want a healthy information system, we need to step up as a profession and work to both limit their power and build healthy alternatives. As long as a very few companies control so many of the materials we need to offer and the software we must use, they will be largely able set their own terms. Combine this with a concomitant attack on the public sector and the funding we all rely on, and the unsustainability of the current system is manifest. There is still competition between companies, of course, but the number of corporations has grown ever smaller over the years and continues to shrink in an ever changing landscape of mergers and acquisitions. And where there is competition, the fundamental alignment of interests remains between corporations, not between corporations and libraries.

Addressing this power imbalance is the most important task we have as a profession because it is the root cause of all other problems. It is a fight that we should lead in our own communities. Unless we stand up to do so, and in doing so claim back much of the control over information that consolidation has cost, the trend toward information becoming a commodity, one that only some people are able to access, will continue unabated. Or even worse, another institution in society will step in to fulfill our traditional role and we will find ourselves left behind, excluded from our most fundamental duty. We are also likely to find that in this process our most vulnerable populations have been excluded from accessing the information they need. At the same time, it is also important for us to fight this fight to preserve what diversity remains in the publishing and library products sector. Small and medium sized companies, nonprofits, and cooperatives are vitally important to the health of the information system, though they struggle in the current environment. By resisting the behemoths, we support these organizations and so improve the health and resiliency of the information system that we rely on. Our job then, the most important job our profession has as a whole, is to re-create the information system anew. To revitalize it so that the possibilities inherent in the technology that we have inherited and built are realized in a way that serves our values and enables us to meet the needs of the 21st century and all of its citizens.

Corporate power in the library and the question of ethics in the relationship between librarians and vendors are closely related, but distinct issues. While I agree fundamentally with John Dupuis in his *Confessions of a Science Librarian* blog, "Our vendors are just that—our vendors. They aren't our friends, they aren't our colleagues, they aren't our patrons, serving them isn't our mission. We aren't on the same side," nonetheless, I do think there is room for nuance there.[1] We may not be able to be friends, but we can certainly be allies. Before delving into the question of how to deal with the behemoths in the room, the giant multinationals whose interests sharply diverge from our own and whose power we need to limit, it is important to acknowledge that libraries need firms. We need someone to produce books and publish journals, we need outside organizations building ILSs that meet a broad range of needs, and we need someone out there making due date stamps and other tools. The people who work in these industries are mostly good people, people who themselves may be as alarmed as we are at the current state of the world and people who may very well share our fundamental values. There are still many successful small and medium sized firms, cooperatives, and nonprofits who desperately need our support and whose products we, in turn, need as badly as they need us to buy those products. This chapter is as much about what we can do to support these companies as it is about dealing with the monopoly power of the big guys in the room. A healthy and sustainable information system is one with a wide range of organizations and where no one organization has so much power that it can harm others.

There are two main paths available to us. The first one is the direct path. This is the path taken when we confront vendors, either directly or through the political system, and when we encourage others to do so. It is the path of advocacy and direct action. This path requires us to use our individual and collective voices to refuse and resist the current system while advocating for reforms and whole new projects that bring us closer to a system that meets the needs of everyone better than the current one. It is not an easy path nor one without controversy, but it is one that has shown considerable success in the past and will serve us well again in the future. The second path is working to build a new system, which usually means supporting open access or open source projects with our expertise, our library dollars and on our campuses. This is the path of building and creating the world we want to live in, the one that we want to hand down to the librarians who come after us. Both of these paths are necessary for us to build a more sustainable library, but neither path alone is sufficient and neither path alone will lead us to where we need to go.

ADVOCACY BY LIBRARY ORGANIZATIONS

Advocacy, speaking publicly about information issues and using the established political system to effect change, has an important role to play in reforming the information system. It is complementary to activism, or nonviolent action. Alone it has limited power, but combined with nonviolent action, it serves an important purpose by articulating the goals and values of the library community both to those in power and to the public at large. The American Library Association and the Association of Research Libraries in particular both have strong histories of advocacy that deserve to be recognized and honored by the profession. *Library Journal* too, with its tireless coverage of legislative issues at all levels, plays an important role as an advocate for libraries. These organizations work within the existing system to build alternatives, promote legislation that serves libraries, share information, and articulate the values of the library community. In doing so, they are an invaluable part of building a new information system.

When looked at as a whole the advocacy that these organizations do is substantive and absolutely vital. The work of the Association of Research Libraries' SPARC in particular has been tireless and effective in building the theoretical and practical basis for a new scholarly communication system based on open access. They formed the Alliance for Taxpayer Access to promote and coordinate support for free access to publicly funded research including the National Institutes of Health Public Access Policy, which was passed in 2009.[2] They have fought successfully against the Research Works Act, a bill that would have banned open access policies for federally funded research, and are currently building support for the FASTR Act, which would require the posting of certain federally funded research within six months of publication.[3] ALA too does good advocacy work, especially for public libraries and at the state level. In 2012, ALA spent $231,275 on lobbyists to advocate directly to Congress.[4] While in an ideal world this would not be necessary, in this world, that work is to be commended and supported. Combined with their support of chapters in each state, the ALA is by far the most powerful group advocating for the needs of libraries and the creation of a healthy information system. They serve as a counterweight to the power of multinational corporations. This work has limitations though and requires support from those who can add nonviolent action into the mix to be successful. These two kinds of activities, advocacy and action in tandem, are how social justice work gets done. It is how to build a successful movement and create lasting change.

NONVIOLENT ACTION

Nonviolent action, with its connotations of militancy and rabble rousing, seems an unlikely tactic to take in rebuilding the information system. Generally, when we think of nonviolent action we think about the civil rights movement or peace activism. The right to information though is a cause that is deeply related to both these causes and just as worthy in its own right. It is one part, an important part, of the much larger struggle for a more just world. More than that, it is our part of the struggle, the part that we as librarians have chosen to be directly involved in day after day, which is why nonviolent action can and should be part of our approach to the current information system. The beauty of nonviolent action is that it includes a far broader range of actions than is generally understood. Gene Sharp, a theorist on nonviolent struggle, has written extensively on the nature of power and resistance. One of his most important observations is that power relies on the cooperation of those who are lower in a hierarchy.[5] It follows then, that by refusing to cooperate with a power structure, it is possible to weaken it. That noncooperation can take many forms; Sharp has identified 198 different forms of nonviolent action, ranging from a strongly worded statement to nonviolent land seizure.[6] Of course, issues of professionalism and decorum put many of these actions off the table for most of us, but even within the bounds of professionalism and proper decorum, there are a far broader range of effective actions available to us and to our patrons than we generally realize.

By examining the history of some recent nonviolent actions by librarians, the scholarly community, and by public library supporters we can see nonviolent action at work within the information system and seek inspiration for future actions that will move us closer to our goals. Not all of these actions have been aimed at corporations, but because tactics are our primary interest here, it is good to look at a wide range of successful campaigns and draw from them what we can. It is also important to acknowledge that in fighting against budget cuts we are fighting against the defunding of the public sphere, which is a core part of building a healthier information system. Three recent actions stand out as effective examples: the actions taken by citizens and librarians in the Save NYC Libraries campaign, the boycott of Elsevier started by Timothy Gowers, and the actions carried out by Aaron Swartz and by his supporters following his death. Each of these was a different kind of action, but each was successful in achieving its goals. Looked at together, they also demonstrate the breadth of actions available to librarians and supporters of libraries.

SAVE NYC LIBRARIES

Even before the collapse of the economy in 2008, New York City libraries were facing serious funding challenges. But after the collapse, the challenges rose quickly to the level of a crisis. In 2009, Mayor Bloomberg's proposal for the 2010–11 fiscal year budget included a 22 percent cut to the Tri-Li, as the public libraries of Manhattan, Brooklyn, and Queens are known, which would have drastically reduced hours and cost almost 1,000 positions.[7] The NYPL fought back with a splash page on their website asking visitors for support and advocates rallied. The Library even produced a celebrity laden YouTube video arguing against the cuts. The group Urban Librarians Unite, previously dedicated to socializing over "beer and tacos," rallied its members and organized a coalition of other library groups including the local library unions, the New York chapter of ACRL, and the local law librarians. They started with a postcard campaign aimed at the city council. Bloomberg responded by reducing the planned cut down to 8 percent.[8] Again though, in 2010, the Tri-Li found itself under the budget knife. In a press release about the cuts NYPL President Paul LeClerc said, "The proposed cut of $36,800,000 is even worse than the cuts to the Library in the 1970s, when New York was on the brink of bankruptcy."[9] And that number does not include the Queen's Public Library or the Brooklyn Public library, each facing cuts of $17 million and $20 million, respectively.[10]

In response, library patrons, activists, and advocates escalated their campaign with a range of actions to both call attention to the planned cuts, but also to communicate the importance of the library in the lives of citizens. The NYPL gave their blessings to Improv Everywhere, a performance art group, who reenacted the scene in the NYPL main reading room from Ghostbusters to raise awareness. The YouTube video took off. It was featured on the front page of YouTube and had been viewed three million times by September of 2010. Urban Librarians Unite and the coalition they helped assemble, now named Save NYC Libraries, held a 24-hour "read-in" in front of the Brooklyn Public Library, the first of what was to become many. The *New York Times* reported on the event and quoted the executive director of Urban Librarians Unite Christian Zabriskie who said, "We librarians have a saying. . . . You can close our libraries when you step over our cold, beaten bodies, chained to the doors."[11] The cuts were reduced and no branches were lost, but again in 2011 the Tri-Li found themselves facing massive cuts.

This time library activists were ready in advance. The proposed cuts for the 2011–2012 fiscal year were 22% and would have resulted in layoffs, reductions in hours, and branch closures.[12] The 24-hour read-in, a letter writing campaign, and a group "hug" around the Swartzman building, the most iconic of the New York City libraries formed the backbone of the action plan. Rallies were also organized at six branch libraries leading up to the 24-hour read-in. The campaigns attracted substantial media coverage and again the libraries of New York City were saved from catastrophic cuts. The next year, in what was becoming an annual event, *Library Journal's* Michael Kelley reported, "New York City Mayor Michael R. Bloomberg presented a $68.7 billion preliminary FY12–13 budget on February 2 that, as usual, proposes Draconian cuts for the city's three library systems."[13] The cuts would have amounted to almost a third of the funding for the Tri-Li. The Save NYC Libraries blog promised, "Big cuts mean big responses. As we get squeezed we push back. Last year we got historic restorations, this year we just have to make bigger history."[14]

And they did. Starting with an event they called the Uni-Read, a reading of the first chapter of the first Harry Potter book in 26 languages, Save NYC Libraries planned a series of events leading up to a larger than ever 24-hour read-in. They followed up the Uni-Read with the distribution of 1,500 "book seeds" across New York. Each book seed was a book with a sticker on the front that read, "Libraries in NYC are facing a 32% budget cut. When libraries close, this could be your only access to free books."[15] The sticker also included a QR Code that linked to a petition citizens could sign. The read-in was a success and again the Mayor blinked and restored most of the cuts. The cuts the next year were larger than ever, at 35 percent of the Tri-Li budget. The Save NYC Libraries blog declared on April 17, "Once more unto the breach . . . Every year we see these kinds of devastating budget cuts and every year we fight like hell and get almost everything back."[16] The 24-hour read-in, now an annual tradition, was well attended, but it was the children's rally at city hall, scheduled to coincide with the arrival of council members for a meeting, that garnered the most attention. Children took to the podium to ask city council members pointed questions about the library budget. The rally was packed and included the presidents of the three impacted library systems, city council members, and many librarians and library supporters. On July 9, the headline on the Save NYC Libraries blog was simply "Victory." All funding had been restored and Save NYC Libraries thanked their supporters, saying, "No Cuts! No Closures! No Layoffs! We did it folks, total budget restoration, and we could not have done it without your help."[17]

ELSEVIER BOYCOTT

The Elsevier boycott began with a single mathematician writing on his blog in January of 2012.[18] That mathematician, Timothy Gowers, summarized his issues with Elsevier's business practices by laying out four areas of objection. First, Gowers wrote, "[Elsevier] charges very high prices—so far above the average that it seems quite extraordinary that they can get away with it." He went on to criticize Elsevier's bundling practices, their negotiating tactics, and their support of the Research Works Act. As a protest against these practices, Gowers decided to make his previous practice of noncooperation public declaring, "So I am not only going to refuse to have anything to do with Elsevier journals from now on, but I am saying so publicly. I am by no means the first person to do this, but the more of us there are, the more socially acceptable it becomes, and that is my main reason for writing this post." He also suggested that it might be useful if there were a place where others who had made the same decision could go public as well. Tyler Neylon, a fellow mathematician, took up this challenge and the website The Cost of Knowledge was born.[19] A Spartan website by most standards, it included little other than a form to complete, some contact information, and an eponymous PDF. Signed by 34 mathematicians, the PDF laid out the argument behind the boycott and called on others to add their names to the list.[20] *Notices of the AMS*, a publication of the American Mathematics Society, followed this up with a set of dueling opinion pieces, one from two of the original signatories of the Cost of Knowledge document and one from Elsevier itself.[21] Three months later, the boycott had more than 10,000 participants and had managed to receive considerable press.[22]

The goals of the boycott varied for each participant, which contributed to the success of the boycott. By not clearly defining the end goals, beyond the basic one of reducing the role that Elsevier plays in scholarly communication, the boycott was able to garner wide appeal. The Cost of Knowledge document said, "Some people would like to see the journal system eliminated completely and replaced by something else more adapted to the internet and the possibilities of electronic distribution. Others see journals as continuing to play a role, but with commercial publishing being replaced by open access models. Still others imagine a more modest change, in which commercial publishers are replaced by non-profit entities such as professional societies . . . or university presses; in this way the value generated by the work of authors, referees, and editors would be returned to the academic and scientific community."[23] While not explicitly stated as a goal of the boycott, the Cost of Knowledge document did criticize Elsevier's support of the Research Works Act, saying, "Recently, Elsevier has lobbied for the Research Works Act, a proposed US law that would undo the National Institutes of Health's public access policy . . . Although most lobbying occurs behind closed doors, Elsevier's vocal support of this act shows their opposition to a popular and effective open access policy."[24] In the opinion piece published in *Notices of the AMS*, Elsevier renounced this support and the legislation died a prompt death. Beyond that though, Elsevier also announced additional concessions. They clarified that authors were permitted to post their work to arXiv, opened backfiles of selected mathematics journals from four years post-publication through 1995, announced a price cut, and declared that "we are open to engaging with the mathematics community on how the system could work better . . . ."[25] By any reasonable standard, the Elsevier boycott has been a phenomenal success, one that demonstrates the power and effectiveness of collective action.

AARON SWARTZ

Aaron Swartz, a young computer expert whose untimely and tragic suicide was certainly the first, and hopefully only, death in the fight for open access, not only carried out direct liberations of inappropriately protected data himself, he also inspired a number of other actions that serve as strong examples of the power of collective nonviolence.[26] Swartz had a long history of direct actions intended to open up the information system. Ranging from his liberation of PACER court documents, to his work with the Library of Congress's database, Swartz was deeply committed to the idea that information, especially public information, should be free and easily accessed. In 2008 he authored the Guerilla Open Access Manifesto. That manifesto declared, "Information is power. But like all power, there are those who want to keep it for themselves. The world's entire scientific and cultural heritage, published over centuries in books and journals, is increasingly being digitized and locked up by a handful of private corporations."[27] He went on to conclude, "We need to take information, wherever it is stored, make our copies and share them with the world. We need to take stuff that's out of copyright and add it to the archive. We need to buy secret databases and put them on the Web. We need to download scientific journals and upload them to file sharing networks. We need to fight for Guerrilla Open Access."[28] His next target was JSTOR.

Why JSTOR? No one knows, but what he did is not in dispute. He went to MIT and used their subscription to download about 4.8 million documents using a simple computer script that ran on a laptop hidden in a closet. He never uploaded these documents and he was fully within his rights to access them via MIT. His arrest and subsequent indictment is where the story takes a dark turn. JSTOR declined to prosecute stating, "It was the government's decision whether to prosecute, not JSTOR's. As noted previously, our interest was in securing the content. Once this was achieved, we had no interest in this becoming an ongoing legal matter."[29] It was the United States Attorney's office that drove the prosecution. They indicted him on four charges: wire fraud, computer fraud, unlawfully obtaining information from a protected computer, and recklessly damaging a protected computer. Later, additional charges were added, including, "breaking and entering, larceny over $250, and unauthorized access to a computer network."[30] Together these charges amounted to $1 million in fines and 35 years in prison. It was the excessive nature of the charges that helped Swartz to gain support. Few people believe that Swartz should not have faced some kind of criminal charge, but if anyone other than the United States Attorney's office believes that $1 million and 35 years in prison for downloading scholarly articles is a just punishment they have been silent.

As his trial neared, his family was working hard to build support within the library community. I know this because I was one of the people who had been asked to write a letter of support for Swartz's nomination for the ALA's James Madison Award. The James Madison Award honors "individuals or groups who have championed, protected and promoted public access to government information and the public's right to know at the national level."[31] Writing that letter and getting the support of my colleagues from the People's Library at Occupy Wall Street was sitting on my to-do list that awful morning after his suicide. The outpouring of support that followed his suicide and the actions that followed are bittersweet. In reacting to the award Swartz's father thanked the library community, saying, "Aaron loved libraries. I remember how excited he was to get library privileges at Harvard and be able to use the Widener library there. I know he would have been humbled and honored to receive this award."[32] Beyond simply raising awareness his death also inspired solidarity actions. In the broader community, the #pdftribute Twitter campaign caught fire with more than 30,000 scholars releasing their work, despite many of them no longer possessing the legal right to do so. JSTOR took the long overdue step of releasing public domain materials to anyone on the web. In a statement JSTOR acknowledged the role that Swartz's death played in this decision: "On a final note, I realize that some people may speculate that making the Early Journal Content free to the public today is a direct response to widely-publicized events over the summer involving an individual who was indicted for downloading a substantial portion of content from JSTOR, allegedly for the purpose of posting it to file sharing sites. While we had been working on releasing the pre-1923/pre-1870 content before the incident took place, it would be inaccurate to say that these events have had no impact on our planning."[33]

Nonviolent action works. It works to inspire, done well it works to build support, and it works by forcing those whose values are abhorrent and petty to show themselves for what they are. It is a necessary complement to the advocacy of library organizations and libraries themselves.

BUILDING AN ALTERNATIVE

Activism and advocacy against the system as it exists are powerful but limited tools. For them to work, there also needs to be a viable alternative, a vision of some sort they are supporting and pushing toward. That vision can be largely theoretical, but it is most powerful when people can see it in action for themselves. When new structures and relationships can be not only imagined, but also experienced, the entire movement is strengthened. In anarchist circles, we call this prefigurative politics. If you have ever heard the old Wobbly slogan "building a new world in the shell of the old," you have heard this idea. Building that new world in the here and now is vital, and it is work that the library community has undertaken enthusiastically. This work demonstrates both the possibilities for what a new information system could look like, and also what is needed to bring that world about.

The caveat though is that this new world that libraries and library organizations have been working to build is still based on carbon polluting technology. An information system built on a combination of open access journals, widely contributed to institutional repositories, and beautifully coded and fully open source ILSs and database software are simply not enough to get us where we need to be. This set of alternatives overlooks vital and serious realities about the world in which we live and the way we fuel that world. As an educator who works with young people, a mother, and someone who is not so old that I expect to check out before the 2C threshold is passed, this is not good enough. Building a new world, creating viable alternatives to the existing one, must be based firmly in reality. Those new systems and new relationships cannot succeed in creating a truly sustainable library without directly confronting and working toward a solution to this problem. It is the elephant in the room, the one we are collectively ignoring. Kari Norgaard is a sociologist who has spent considerable time exploring the question of why and knowledge of climate change, a basic understanding of which requires only knowing that carbon dioxide warms the planet and that fossil fuel burning emits carbon dioxide in large amounts, has not been enough to create a serious movement for social change.[34] She identifies both causes and mechanisms that we use, collectively, to suppress discussion and action. These are mechanisms that we can see at work in our own community and finding a way past them is absolutely required if we are to build a genuinely sustainable library. That is the task of the final chapter of this book.

NOTES

1. John Dupuis, "Library Vendors, Politics, Aaron Swartz, #pdftribute." *Confessions of a Science Librarian*, *ScienceBlogs*, http://scienceblogs.com/confessions/2013/01/17/library-vendors-politics-aaron-swartz-pdftribute.

2. "National Institutes of Health Public Access Policy," Alliance for Taxpayer Access, accessed December 12, 2013, www.taxpayeraccess.org/issues/nih/index.shtml.

3. "Who Opposes the Fair Copyright in Research Works Act," Alliance for Taxpayer Access, accessed December 13, 2013, www.taxpayeraccess.org/issues/opposition/index.shtml.

4. "American Library Assn.," Center for Responsive Politics, accessed December 12, 2013, www.opensecrets.org/lobby/clientsum.php?id=D000046971&year=2012.

5. Gene Sharp, *The Politics of Nonviolent Action: Part One, Power and Struggle* (Boston: Porter Sargent, 1973).

6. Gene Sharp, *The Politics of Nonviolent Action: Part Two, The Methods of Nonviolent Action* (Boston: Porter Sargent, 1973).

7. Michael Rogers et al., "In NYC, 22% Proposed Library Budget Cut," *Library Journal* 134, no. 10 (2009): 12.

8. New York City Public Library, "Annual Report: Report of the Treasurer," (2009).

9. "New York Public Library Faces Harshest Budget Cut in Its History," *Art Daily*, May 8, 2010, http://artdaily.com/news/37928/New-York-Public-Library-Faces-Harshest-Budget-Cut-In-Its-History#.UoUHSiRQ2Ho.

10. Maya Pope-Chappell, "N.Y. Librarians Fight Budget Cuts, Pledge 'We Will Not Be Shushed,'" Metropolis, *Wall Street Journal*, http://blogs.wsj.com/metropolis/2010/06/14/ny-librarians-fight-budget-cuts-pledge-we-will-not-be-shushed.

11. Michael M. Grynbaum, "24-Hour Read-in Protests Cuts to Libraries," *New York Times*, June 13, 2010, www.nytimes.com/2010/06/14/nyregion/14shush.html?_r=0.

12. "New Library Cuts for FY'12," Save NYC Libraries, February 22, 2011, www
    .savenyclibraries.com/?p=319.

13. Michael Kelley, "Bloomberg Proposes Cutting NYC Library Funding by Nearly
    $100 Million," *Library Journal* (February 8, 2012), http://lj.libraryjournal
    .com/2012/02/opinion/john-berry/bloomberg-proposes-cutting-library
    -funding-by-nearly-100-million.

14. "To the Stacks!" Save NYC Libraries, February 13, 2012, www.savenyclibraries
    .com/?p=676.

15. Save NYC Libraries, "Book Seeding in NYC," news release, *Liswire,* May 21,
    2012, http://liswire.com/content/book-seeding-nyc.

16. Save NYC Libraries, "Once More Unto the Breach!" April 17, 2013, www
    .savenyclibraries.com/?p=1010.

17. Save NYC Libraries, "Victory," July 9, 2013, www.savenyclibraries.com/?p
    =1148.

18. Timothy Gowers, "Elsevier—My Part in Its Downfall." *Gowers's Weblog:
    Mathematics Related Discussions,* http://gowers.wordpress.com/2012/01/21/
    elsevier-my-part-in-its-downfall.

19. Tyler Neylon, "The Cost of Knowledge," December 13, 2013, http://
    thecostofknowledge.com.

20. Ibid.

21. Douglas N. Arnold and Henry Cohn, "Mathematicians Take a Stand," *Notices of
    the AMS* 59, no. 6 (2012): 828–33; Laura Hassinik and David Clark, "Elsevier's
    Response to the Mathematics Community," *Notices of the AMS* 59, no. 6
    (2012): 833–35.

22. Tyler Neylon, "Life after Elsevier: Making Open Access to Scientific Knowledge
    a Reality," *Guardian,* www.theguardian.com/science/blog/2012/apr/24/life
    -elsevier-open-access-scientific-knowledge.

23. Neylon, "The Cost of Knowledge."

24. Ibid.

25. David Clark, "Mathematical Publishing, Part III: Elsevier's Response to 'the
    Cost of Knowledge,'" London Mathematical Society newsletter, no. 412
    (March 2012) http://old.lms.ac.uk/newsletter/412/412_issue.pdf.

26. I am friends and neighbors with the family of Aaron Swartz's partner, Taren
    Stinebrickner-Kauffman.

27. Aaron Swartz, "Guerilla Open Access Manifesto," http://ia600808.us.archive
    .org/17/items/GuerillaOpenAccessManifesto/Goamjuly2008.pdf.

28. Ibid.

29. JSTOR, "JSTOR Statement: Misuse Incident and Criminal Case," news release,
    July 19, 2011, http://about.jstor.org/news/jstor-statement-misuse-incident
    -and-criminal-case.

30. John A. Hawkinson, "Swartz Indicted for Breaking and Entering," *The Tech*
    (MIT newspaper), November 18, 2011.

31. "James Madison Award," American Library Association, accessed December 13, 2013, www.ala.org/awardsgrants/james-madison-award.

32. Julie Bort, "The American Library Association Has Given Aaron Swartz Its First Ever Posthumous Award," *Business Insider*, March 15, 2013, www .businessinsider.com/aaron-swartz-granted-posthumous-award-2013-3.

33. Laura Brown, "JSTOR—Free Access to Early Journal Content and Serving 'Unaffiliated' Users," JSTOR, news release, September 7, 2011, http://about .jstor.org/news/jstor%E2%80%93free-access-early-journal-content-and -serving-%E2%80%9Cunaffiliated%E2%80%9D-users.

34. Kari Norgaard, *Living in Denial: Climate Change, Emotions, and Everyday Life* (Cambridge, MA: MIT Press, 2011).

9
Resolving the Technology Dilemma

Climate change and technology are intimately linked for the library community, because technology is where we are the most responsible for carbon emissions. Any attempt to define and implement a sustainable library or a vision of what sustainable librarianship should look like cannot be successful unless the challenges, both technical and ethical, that derive from the realities of carbon pollution are confronted head on. But doing so is deeply difficult, not simply because it is a big question to answer, but also because we have social norms that direct us away from this question. We live in a state of denial about the reality of the task in front of us. Kari Norgaard, a sociologist, looked at this question, the question of why we live in denial about what climate change means for us and identified how this process works in society.[1] In her case, she was examining a small Norwegian town, but she also applied her analysis to the United States. What she found was that knowledge of climate change made people feel sad and uncomfortable. It evoked feelings of fear, guilt, and helplessness. It threatened their identity and their understanding of themselves as "a good person." She also found that two different types of denial were in play. The first is literal denial and it is pervasive in the United States. Literal denial, the creation of it and how it is sustained, was well covered by Naomi Oreskes and Erik M. Conway in their book *Merchants of Doubt*.[2] They documented the ongoing and alarmingly successful attempts by industry and their partners in free-market think tanks to sow denial and cast doubt on the established scientific consensus on climate change. As librarians, who have a strong history of respect for scholarship and academic honesty, literal denial is not something we struggle with in our own professional community. It is the second kind of denial, implicatory denial, that we face.

Implicatory denial was also the kind of denial that Norgaard found at work in Norway. In implicatory denial a set of facts are not in contention, rather it is the reaction to those facts, what those facts mean in terms of feelings and actions, that are at issue.[3] Norgaard looked at how implicatory denial is implemented through norms and conventions and found that there were specific strategies at play. The first set of norms she identified were conversational norms, norms about what we talk about and what we do not talk about.[4] In her research she found that there was no social or even political space to discuss climate change in the small Norwegian town that she used as a case study. It wasn't an appropriate topic of conversation for small talk, it wasn't on the agenda at local political meetings, because it was seen as a national issue, and in educational settings the expectation of optimism kept serious talk about climate off the table. The library community too has this norm. A search in LISTA reveals that when you search for "climate change" AND "United States" and cut out reviews, only 43 articles are returned since 2000 and hardly any of those actually talk about libraries and climate change. Conferences too fail to provide conversational space for discussions about climate change. Not once has there been a session at ALA Annual or Midwinter about what librarians can do to address carbon pollution in the information system, and no other conference that I am aware of has addressed the issue either. If there is an ongoing conversation about how libraries need to work to restructure the information system to adapt to a carbon free economy, it seems to be taking place very quietly and without widespread participation. Like in Norgaard's Norwegian town, climate change is simply not a topic of conversation in our professional discourse. It is almost entirely absent.

Beyond conversational norms, Norgaard identified emotional norms that kept climate change off the agenda.[5] As she put it, "Feelings such as guilt or helplessness are not only unpleasant to experience, but also inappropriate to reveal publicly; they are emotions that cultural norms bar from public expression."[6] Talking about climate change, in any way beyond the superficial, means talking about and experiencing emotions. It means revealing oneself to be not in full control of one's emotional state, in that reacting to climate change is always, at its root, a moral and emotional reaction. As in Norgaard's town, within the library community it means being seen as less than serious, because serious people do not talk about climate change, much less about doing anything about the problem. Talking about climate change is a marginalizing activity, one that situates the speaker outside the mainstream. In the library community, serious people talk about budgets, new technology, new products. They talk about open access and open source projects. They do not talk about the fact that all of that wonderful technology is also responsible for contributing to the atmospheric release of 20 million gigatons of carbon per year by the high tech industry.[7] They do not talk about moral culpability and making decisions that account for the complex ethical issues surrounding climate change. The topic is too emotional, too distant from the concerns that we have defined as legitimate. It is simply not done in polite circles.

This brings us to Norgaard's final explanation, norms of attention. Cultural norms of attention tell us what is important and what we should think about. They direct our attention toward or away from certain topics. Climate change is an area where our cultural norm is to ignore the topic within the context of our own work. Norgaard found that this was also the case in her town. Time and space played a vital role there, as they do for us. As a profession we are very future focused, but that future, the one we envision for ourselves, rarely extends out more than five years. Even when we talk of the distant future, we rarely go beyond 20 or 25 years. Our norms of attention also keep us tightly focused on the information realm, and not on the relationship between that realm and the wider world. We do not pay attention to questions of server hardware, energy use within the information system as a whole, or questions of our profession's ethical duty to the larger world. When we do talk about ethics, we keep them firmly within the range of what is understood as information ethics, and not on wider questions of our responsibility to larger notions of justice. We have defined climate change as outside of our professional realm, as not our problem to address.

Norgaard's work focuses on the why and the how of climate change inaction within society, but that is only part of the story. To work our way out of the problem, we also have to consider what about the problem itself makes climate such an intractable issue. What specific challenges does climate present that make us so reluctant to take it up seriously? Donald Brown, a climate change ethicist, has written extensively about the problem of inaction on climate. So has Stephen Gardiner, who produced a book titled *A Perfect Moral Storm: The Ethical Tragedy of Climate Change*, where he lays out an explanation for why climate change is so hard to fix. In his case, he was talking about the international and national institutions who are supposed to be addressing the problem, but it applies across all levels. He identifies three main barriers that make the problem hard to fix. The first is the "dispersion of causes and effects."[8] Because climate impacts are so distant from their causes, it can be hard to see the action, emitting carbon dioxide, as related to the impact, whether that impact is drought or flood or rising sea levels. This makes changing behavior especially challenging. The second barrier he identifies is what he calls the "fragmentation of agency," in other words, the fact that no one person or group is responsible.[9] Rather, it is the collective emissions that are responsible, which means that blame can only be incompletely and partially assigned. Because blame can only be partially assigned, changing behavior becomes more challenging. The third barrier is "institutional inadequacy."[10] Both at the international and national level, the institutions who should work to solve this problem are not structured to do so, lacking both legitimacy and authority. Repeated failures, from the Kyoto Protocol to the utter mess that was the Copenhagen Climate Change Conference have more than demonstrated that. We simply have no international governance in place that can manage the challenges that climate change presents. While Gardiner's book is truly the best discussion of the problem of inaction on climate, he makes no real attempt to offer solutions. It is Donald Brown's book, *Climate Change Ethics: Navigating the Perfect Moral Storm*, in which a serious attempt at a way out of the problem is offered.

Brown's book was inspired by Gardiner's and takes up where he left off, with ethical explanations that point the way out of the "perfect moral storm."[11] Much of the book is dedicated to what national governments and international governance organizations should do and why they should do it, but he also addresses the responsibilities of subnational governments and other organizations. Brown dismisses the idea that climate change is solely the domain of national governments and international organizations, writing, "Given the magnitude of the emissions reductions needed worldwide to prevent potentially catastrophic climate change, the world is unlikely to make the huge reductions necessary to prevent dangerous warming unless all sub-national governments, organizations and businesses, and individuals accept their moral responsibility to reduce emissions to their fair share of safe global emissions."[12] He also points out, drawing on the work of Paul Harris, that much of the emphasis on state level actors has served as a distraction, directing attention away from those who do the bulk of the emitting. After all, while national governments certainly emit carbon as part of their own activities, the bulk of emissions come from businesses and other actors. Harris makes this point particularly well, stating, "Far from being a solution to environmental problems, international justice in the context of climate change has been at best a justification for giving developing states a bit more aid, which they deserve, but has if anything been a kind of 'curse' that has preoccupied diplomats and prevented them from seriously and fully discussing the role of people per se as causes of climate change, thus avoiding where the source of the problem really lies—with the people who actually cause the most pollution and are capable of reducing it."[13] Brown builds on this idea, concluding, "Because regional and local governments, organizations, businesses and individuals are responsible for greenhouse gas emissions that have caused, and will continue to cause, harm to others, all have responsibilities to limit their harmful emissions without regard to whether their nation has acted."[14] For us in libraries, this means that we do have a moral obligation to attend to the emissions that we rely on to do our work. It means that climate change is our problem and deserves our attention.

Before delving into the question of what to do, looking for a moment at the science behind climate change can give us a sense of the scope of the problem, of what the scale of needed change is to avoid catastrophic impacts. Bill McKibben's 2012 *Rolling Stone* article spoke to this issue in a particularly clear and unique way. He identified three important numbers for the climate movement: 2, 565, and 2,795. The 2 refers to the shaky but long-standing goal of keeping global temperature increases below 2°C.[15] The 565 refers to the gigatons of carbon dioxide scientists say we can emit before we reach that 2 degree limit. Remember that every year we emit about 31 gigatons of carbon dioxide.[16] This has historically increased by about 3 percent per year, giving us about 13 years left—if we want to burn through our carbon budget like a drunk shopper on Amazon. The 2,795 refers to the number of gigatons of carbon currently sitting on the books of fossil fuel interests. As McKibben puts it, "We have five times as much oil and coal and gas on the books as climate scientists think is safe to burn. We'd have to keep 80 percent of those reserves locked away underground to avoid that fate.[17] Any hope that we can manage that without a widespread social movement and without everyone doing everything they can to transform our economy and our morality is optimistic to the point of delusion. In the words of civil rights activist turned climate leader and pastor Dr. Gerald Durley, "Our success rests on the willingness of all of us—all races, creeds, and walks of life—coming together with a single purpose."[18] This is our fight, because this is everyone's fight.

WHAT TO DO

Accepting that climate change is our problem and that we do have an obligation to act to build an information system that is not dependent on carbon polluting infrastructure is the first step. The second is deciding what to do about the problem. The question of what to do as employees, in our own libraries, has already been covered in chapter 4, but that leaves us with the larger information system and what to do about those emissions. None of us wants to "throw the baby out with the bath water," so we cannot simply turn our backs and do without this system. Instead, we must work for reforms. Fortunately, we have a toolkit to do that already, one that we have had years to refine and develop: advocacy and activism. Historically, we have had great success with these kinds of campaigns, as we saw in chapter 8. We can use those same techniques and build that same kind of relationship between advocates and activists to fight this fight too. We just have to make the decision to do so and to give it the same energy that we have given to the struggle for open access and open source software. By changing the terms of that debate, by incorporating a broader vision of sustainability into our existing movement for change, we can leverage the success we have had in one area to ensure that we are successful in the fight for clean technology too.

The fight for clean technology is different from our fight against the enclosure of the information commons in ways that deserve to be spelled out so that we can consider them carefully. First, as urgent as the battle against enclosure has been, that urgency pales in comparison with climate. Scientists tell us that we needed to have begun a massive reduction in our emissions decades ago. We have no real time left to dither on this one. The point at which catastrophic impacts become unavoidable may have already passed. There is simply no time left in this fight. At the same time though, while open access puts us at odds with our vendors, climate is an issue where we should be on the same side. Being powered by fossil fuels instead of clean energy is not fundamental to their business models. Our vendors are also facing rising prices for energy and climate impacts. They have no real reason not to convert to clean energy, especially if they can show their shareholders that their customers are serious about change. Even the monopolistic information vendors can join us on this one. If they choose, they can make the decision to invest in their own future by converting to clean technology and in doing so strengthen their companies. But this will cost money for them; there is no way to deny that. So they need our support. They need to know that this is important to us and that we will not back off until they can demonstrate that they have made real changes, not simply added a layer of greenwashing over their marketing.

This brings us to the biggest difference. A healthy and resilient information system is made up of all kinds of organizations, profit seeking firms, nonprofit organizations, cooperatives. There is room for a wide range of information vendors and a healthy system would have a good mix of all of these. The problem in the information system has been an overgrowth and a concentration of power by one segment. We need change, yes, but what we need there is a rebalancing, a reformation. The kind of change needed to get us off fossil fuels is going to require something more akin to a revolution. Not a political revolution, but something closer to a second industrial revolution. It will require a serious rethinking of what we use energy for, how we get that energy, and what costs we are willing to incur along the way. It requires us to begin thinking in starkly moral terms about things that have become second nature to us, things like driving a car or turning on a light. It will require us to forgo money that could be made by digging up and selling coal and tar sands.

It will almost certainly require us to learn how to live on less energy, possibly much less energy. The difference in magnitude between the kind of change required to convert to a clean energy economy and the kind of change required to rebuild a healthy information system is enormous. But fortunately, we have allies across the information world and across the entire world. This is a much bigger fight, but there are so many more people fighting it with us. We do not have to go this one alone.

LIBRARY ADVOCACY ORGANIZATIONS

The movement for a clean energy and a fossil fuel free library and information system is only just beginning, but it has started. To build a successful movement, we will need to get both the large traditional advocacy organizations and smaller activist groups involved. We will probably need to form new activist groups as well. We have to open up a space within our professional discourse for conversation on the topic by holding conferences, making presentations at established conferences, and contributing to the professional literature. Incorporating climate into the discourse on the future of libraries and adding clean technology to the agenda will also require us to attract new members to these groups and build a new energy. It will require reaching out to those who have traditionally felt marginalized in the mainstream library community and encouraging them to raise their voices and insist on being accepted as legitimate participants. This is an enormous task, but we have a strong history of this kind of work to build on and well-honed tools available to us.

The library advocacy groups, ALA, ARL, and groups like SLA and AALL are well placed to contribute to that effort and to provide both venues and a certain level of legitimacy to the conversation. ALA has already started moving in this direction with the founding of the Sustainability Roundtable and the Council's adoption of the Resolution on the Divestment of Holdings in Fossil Fuel Companies. The Progressive Librarians' Guild has also adopted a version of this Resolution. In addition, there was also the Sustainability in Libraries online conference in 2012. So we are moving in the right direction as a community. But there is still much more we need to do to get a movement off the ground, into libraries, and out to our vendors.

As a first step in that direction, we could follow the lead of other professional organizations like the American Public Health Association and the American Academy of Pediatrics by adopting a strongly worded statement about the importance of solving the problem of climate change and mitigating the unavoidable consequences. Most of these statements follow a similar pattern. The American Public Health Association's statement is a good example. It starts by acknowledging the problem, "Current best estimates project that global temperatures will increase by 1.8 to 4.0°C by 2100, and sea levels may rise 0.18 to 0.59 m or more this century, depending on ice sheet dynamics. Scientists calculate that significant reductions in GHG emissions must begin to take place within 10 years for humans to have a chance at averting dangerous climate change."[19] It goes on to call for specific actions that the public health community should undertake, including "advocate for mitigation and avoidance of climate change, track the impacts of climate change on human health, and assist with adaptation, to the degree possible, to those health effects caused by changes in climate that cannot be prevented . . . Acknowledge that freedom from serious adverse effects of global climate change qualifies as a basic human right as the APHA understands that term."[20] It also calls on public health professionals themselves to "adopt practices that minimize GHG emissions related to their activities."[21] Library organizations should adopt similar statements that could serve as a way for librarians both within their institutions and within the information system as whole to unify their responses. Just as we point to the ALA's Right to Read statement and the Information Bill of Rights, a climate statement would provide us a set of professional expectations and obligations to follow in our own work. It could serve as the basis for advocacy with our vendors and with our home institutions. Alone, strongly worded statements cannot make any changes, but they can serve as the basis for action.

Before we turn to action, it is worthwhile to consider what our advocacy organizations could do beyond statements. Much like library directors, advocacy organizations face limitations on what they can do to encourage social change. They are obligated to work within the existing system to effect change and to be cautious of not offending their members and supporters. That said, they also bring to the table considerable organizational and mobilization strengths that can be brought to bear on social problems. One way to leverage this strength would be for the large advocacy organizations to collaborate and follow the model of the American College and University Presidents' Climate Commitment. The Presidents' Climate Commitment has been signed by 677 college and university presidents and chancellors. Funded by Second Nature, a nonprofit organized to promote sustainability in higher education, the Commitment is intended to offer higher education institutions a way to both provide leadership and collaborate on climate issues. As the FAQ states, "The threat of catastrophic climate disruption, is not 'just another' issue. The scale and magnitude of addressing this common crisis in an effective and timely manner, through redesigning the basic mechanisms by which we meet our needs, requires purposeful collective action, and will require unprecedented modes of collaboration."[22] The Commitment itself begins by identifying the problem and its severity, "We, the undersigned presidents and chancellors of colleges and universities, are deeply concerned about the unprecedented scale and speed of global warming and its potential for large-scale, adverse health, social, economic and ecological effects."[23] Then it goes on to enumerate the causes and what must be done, "We further recognize the need to reduce the global emission of greenhouse gases by 80% by mid-century at the latest."[24] It follows that with a multipoint plan that colleges and universities signing the Commitment agree to enact. For the library community, a similar Commitment could take two forms. One route would be to create such a commitment for library directors to sign about their own libraries. Alternatively, and I think perhaps more wisely, we could create a commitment for our vendors to sign. A model like this one would offer good opportunities for collaboration and cooperation for our vendors, the organizations themselves, and the movement for clean technology in libraries.

LIBRARY ACTIVISM

Strongly worded statements and promises to do better are not going to solve this problem by themselves. Rather their role is to help provide support for those, both in libraries and among our vendors, who are working for change. As we saw with the fight for open access, social movements need both advocates and activists working together to be successful. Neither alone can create social change. Fortunately, librarians have a long and proud history of social activism to draw on in this fight, to complement the work of our advocacy groups and to push them along in their work. From the refusal of Zoia Horn to testify against an antiwar activist to Ruth Brown's loss of her position for her dedication to service to the African-American community to Juliette Morgan and her role in the Montgomery bus boycott, librarians have been active, as librarians, in every major social movement of the past century. Adding our voices and our bodies to this fight, and directing them toward our own emissions is both the right moral choice and one firmly based in who we are as a profession. But how do we do it? What steps do we need to take to build a strong activist movement for a clean information system?

Obviously, this is much bigger question than can be answered here and it is one that we need to come together as a community to work out. Many people will need to work together to plan actions and sort out a direction for a library based climate movement. As a start though, we can begin by lending our support to the existing climate movement. Nonviolent climate activism outside of the library world has been growing and showing increasing success in both delaying carbon-based infrastructure projects and raising awareness. Library organizations like Radical Reference are already offering their support to these groups, but we can do more by participating in these actions as a group, by coming out to marches and sit-ins as librarians and reporting back to the library community so that our actions have visibility. We are also well suited to join in and organize book bloc actions as part of marches and protests. Book blocs are a new nonviolent tactic that started in Europe and are growing in popularity here in the United States. The basic idea behind a book bloc is for people to lead marches with the covers of powerful books enlarged and turned into shields. As a tactic it communicates the larger ideals behind an action, while at the same time evoking a powerful connection with the love of literacy and reading that our own profession embodies. We can also create mobile libraries and join actions in the explicit role of librarian. By offering relevant literature, usually collected from sympathetic publishers and donations, we can be in the midst of an action doing what we do best, serving patrons. Actions like this can be combined with activism for public library funding and open access projects too. By showing up as ourselves and doing the work we do, we are contributing to the climate movement in the best way we can.

We also need to bring the movement home to the information system too. Organizing nonconfrontational climate awareness actions to coincide with major conferences and that target our vendors is a good starting point. We have done virtually nothing as a profession to communicate to vendors how important it is that they take responsibility for their emissions. A rally or other awareness raising action at a conference can serve as a first volley, a way of saying, "this matters to us and we need you to change." By coordinating with advocacy groups and offering something like the Presidents' Climate Commitment, we could offer them a framework for action that they can begin implementing. We can offer them a way forward out of this mess. Unless vendors see us out there, see that we are serious about the need for change and about our refusal to continue to participate in a system that causes grave harm, they will not change. The same goes for open access and open source projects, unless we work to put clean technology on the agenda, they will not have the support they need to follow through on creating a truly sustainable library. It is only by unifying our voices and raising them together that we can pull others along with us. Practicing sustainable librarianship requires us to do nothing less.

NOTES

1. Kari Norgaard, *Living in Denial: Climate Change, Emotions, and Everyday Life* (Cambridge, MA: MIT Press, 2011).
2. Naomi Oreskes and Erik M. Conway, *Merchants of Doubt: How a Handful of Scientists Obscured the Truth on Issues from Tobacco Smoke to Global Warming*, 1st US ed. (New York: Bloomsbury Press, 2010).
3. Norgaard, *Living in Denial*, 10–11.
4. Ibid., 97–105.

5. Ibid., 106–12.

6. Ibid., 106.

7. "Emissions of Greenhouse Gases in the United States 2009," US Energy Information Administration, Department of Energy (Washington, DC, March 2011).

8. Stephen M. Gardiner, *A Perfect Moral Storm: The Ethical Tragedy of Climate Change* (New York: Oxford University Press, 2011), 24.

9. Ibid.

10. Ibid.

11. Donald A. Brown, *Climate Change Ethics: Navigating the Perfect Moral Storm* (Abingdon, UK: Routledge, 2013).

12. Ibid., 196.

13. Paul G. Harris, *World Ethics and Climate Change: From International to Global Justice* (Edinburgh: Edinburgh University Press, 2010), 93.

14. Brown, *Climate Change Ethics: Navigating the Perfect Moral Storm*, 201.

15. Bill McKibben, "Global Warming's Terrifying New Math," *Rolling Stone*, no. 1162 (2012), www.rollingstone.com/politics/news/global-warmings -terrifying-new-math-20120719.

16. Miriam Quick, Ella Hollowood, and David McCandless, "How Many Gigatons of Carbon Dioxide? The Information Is Beautiful Guide to Doha," *DataBlog*, *Guardian*, www.theguardian.com/news/datablog/2012/dec/07/carbon-dioxide -doha-information-beautiful#_.

17. McKibben, "Global Warming's Terrifying New Math."

18. Rev. Dr. Gerald Durley, "Why Climate Change Is a Civil Rights Issue," HuffPost, Black Voices, www.huffingtonpost.com/rev-dr-gerald-durley/climate -change-civil-rights_b_3844986.html?.

19. "Addressing the Urgent Threat of Global Climate Change to Public Health and the Environment," American Public Health Association, November 6, 2007, www.apha.org/advocacy/policy/policysearch/default.htm?id=1351.

20. Ibid.

21. Ibid.

22. "Frequently Asked Questions," American College & University Presidents' Climate Commitment, accessed April 24, 2014, www.presidentsclimatecom mitment.org/about/faqs.

23. "Text of the American College & University Presidents' Climate Commitment," American College & University Presidents' Climate Commitment, accessed April 24, 2014, www.presidentsclimatecommitment.org/about/commitment.

24. Ibid.

10
Visioning the Sustainable Library

onella Meadows was a brilliant systems scientist and an activist for sustainability, for a world infused with environmental, economic, and social justice. She tells a story about running a workshop for adults on eliminating world hunger. The participants were all very serious professionals across a range of hunger-related fields including agronomists, nutritionists, and economists, working in positions that required them to think deeply about the topic of world hunger. She started her workshop by asking them, "to describe not the world they thought they could achieve, or the world they were willing to settle for, but the world they truly wanted."[1] To her surprise, the group grew angry. They resisted her request fiercely.

She quotes the participants at length:

- Visions are fantasies; they don't change anything. Talking about them is a waste of time. We don't need to talk about what the end of hunger will be like, we need to talk about how to get there.
- We all know what it's like not to be hungry. What's important to talk about is how terrible it is to be hungry.
- I never really thought about it. I'm not sure what the world would be like without hunger, and I don't see why I need to know.

- Stop being unrealistic. There will always be hunger. We can decrease it, but we can never eliminate it.
- You have to be careful with visions. They can be dangerous. Hitler had a vision. I don't trust visionaries and I don't want to be one.

Eventually, she worked through the objections with the group and she concluded that the fundamental objection was this: "I have a vision, but it would make me feel childish and vulnerable to say it out loud. I don't know you all well enough to do this."[2]

Imagining the world we want, whether at work or in the broader realm, can feel silly and it certainly makes us all feel vulnerable. Librarians in particular have a habit of practicality. We have no real space to talk about the world we want and no social traditions of doing so. Vision lives at the edges of our world. Conferences talk about the "library of the future," but it is always a practical exercise, one that focuses on managing new technologies. We may talk about what a fully digital library would look like, but is it always a question of how to cope with this world we are being steered toward, not what we would want it to be like. We may talk about social justice issues in the library, but always as a practical matter for library services and collections. As a profession, we see ourselves largely at the mercy of outside forces that we have limited control over and which determine our future. We do not share our dreams. We do not publicly imagine. We do not offer big visions for the information system beyond those that come from technology that we do not control. We are a practical group, firmly rooted in the possible and the here and now.

This book is a challenge to that identity. To the idea that good librarianship is only a practical and largely technical activity. To the idea that librarians should work with the world as it is without pushing back and trying to mold it into what we want it to be. To the idea that librarianship lacks theory and that the only theory that matters is information science. Meadows goes on to write about the importance of vision, "If we can't speak of our real desires, we can only marshal information, models, and implementation toward what we think we can get, not toward what we really want. We only half-try . . . . That sets up a positive feedback loop spiraling downward. The less we try, the less we achieve. The less we achieve, the less we try."[3] We have been endlessly guilty of this as a profession. We have not always recognized the power of imagination and our own power to enact the world we want. But we can change that. We can all look around our libraries and look around the information system we rely on and imagine what we would like to see. We can imagine a world with well-funded libraries, an information system with responsive vendors whose focus is not on the bottom line but on a healthy information system. We can imagine our relationships in the library being built on trust and mutual respect. We can imagine all of our colleagues with a living wage and access to health care. We can look around at what we do in our communities and imagine that the value of our work is recognized and rewarded. Unless we do that, unless we have a vision for what a library should be and what the information system should look like, we will not be able to build the library and information system we want. We will not be able to serve our communities in the way our shared values call on us to serve. Vision gives us a goal, it gives us motivation, and it gives meaning to our professional lives.

Vision is particularly important in times of change and we live in one of those times right now. Not simply technological change, which is the kind of change librarians usually talk about when we talk change, but much larger social and environmental changes too. From the ongoing project to defund public services, to the transformation from a manufacturing into a service economy, to changes in higher education that move it toward a more corporate model; changes in the larger world impact both our information system and the kinds of materials and services we need to offer. They challenge our internal organization and the skills we need to bring to the table to serve our communities most effectively. They challenge our relationships with our vendors and the structure of the companies we rely on. The most important of all of these though, is climate change. The most recent IPCC report predicts a 1.4°C to 2.4°C temperature rise in my lifetime.[4] For my daughter, now five, it predicts a 2.1°C–4.5°C increase. Given that 2°C is widely understood to be the level at which we risk severe and long-term consequences and since we have already increased the temperature by about .8°C, this means that at some point in my career the impacts of climate change are likely to be felt in my library. Ignoring this physical reality or leaving dealing with the consequences to the future is not a responsible decision. It is not a moral decision. It is not a decision that serves my values, my patrons, or my own future.

Vision without a grounding in reality is of no use to anyone. Visions must take into account the physical reality of the world in which we all live. Meadows puts it this way: "Vision is not rational, BUT rational mind can and must inform vision. . . . I use every rational tool at my disposal not to weaken the basic values behind my vision, but to shape it into a responsible vision that acknowledges, but doesn't get crushed by, the physical constraints of the world."[5] Vision, then, must be tempered with reality. It must be based on a true understanding of the world, while remaining firmly rooted in a moral sense of what that world should be. It must also be shared. As Meadows explains it, "One essential tool for making vision responsible is sharing it with others and incorporating their visions. Only shared vision can be responsible."[6] This combination, a grounding in reality and building a vision shared by the community, constitutes responsible visioning, which is what the library community needs to engage in and quickly if we want to have a chance of enacting that vision.

This book is my attempt at responsible visioning, at opening a dialog for what kind of future we want to have as a profession and how we want to get there. One of the core ideas of the sustainability movement is that the future will not look like the past. The future is going to be different, it might be much worse if we do not attend to the problems we are creating. But it also has the potential to be much, much better. I started this book the year I turned 30. Turning 30 is a good way to start feeling like a real adult. That same year, a dear staff member was diagnosed with breast cancer. For me, the combination of the two events brought home the fact that I was one of the adults in the room finally and that that meant I was now responsible for the world I handed down to my newborn daughter. It made me realize that my time is limited and I have an obligation to use it well. I first learned about climate change when I was in the fifth grade. I remember thinking to myself that I was glad we had learned about the problem now, so that it would be solved by the time I was an adult. It never occurred to my ten-year-old self that I would reach adulthood and the problem would remain unsolved. That it would become a problem for me, one that I would someday have to explain to my own ten-year-old. But here we are.

We have no excuses not to build the world we want. We have the tools, social activism and advocacy. We all have voices we can use and the time to use them is now. I do not want my own children to reach adulthood and find that I have left them a mess through my own inaction and no one else does either. A better world is possible, but only if we fight for it with everything we have. Only if we take the legacy of those who fought before us and emulate their bravery and tenacity. We have a long storied history as a profession and it is our turn to continue the struggle that those who came before us fought so that we would be here to fight this one. It is time to honor that legacy and our profession's most deeply held values by building a library and information system we can be to proud hand down to the librarians of future generations.

NOTES

1. Donella Meadows, "Envisioning a Sustainable World," October 8, 2012, www.donellameadows.org/archives/envisioning-a-sustainable-world.
2. Ibid.
3. Ibid.
4. To calculate for yourself: www.theguardian.com/environment/interactive/2013/sep/27/climate-change-how-hot-lifetime-interactive.
5. Meadows, "Envisioning a Sustainable World."
6. Ibid.

Sustainability Assessment Worksheet

Document Gathering

Gather the following documents as part of the process:

- Institutional Vision Statement
- Library Vision Statement
- Institutional Mission Statement
- Library Mission Statement
- Institutional Sustainability Vision Statement
- Library Sustainability Vision Statement

THE ASSESSMENT TOOL—PART 1

1. The sustainability committee
   a. Is there one?
   b. If not, does one make sense for this library?
   c. Who should serve on the committee?
   d. How can it include members from across the library hierarchy and system?

    e. How often should it plan to meet, and what are its immediate goals?

    f. Who from outside the library should it include?

    g. What about branch libraries?

    h. How does it fit into the larger library committee structure?

    i. Does the committee have a written mission or vision?

    j. What is the process for setting objectives and informing the library about its activities?

2. Support for sustainability initiatives

    a. Does the committee or person completing the assessment believe that the library administration is supportive of transitioning to a more sustainable model?

    b. What about the city or university administration?

    c. Does the city or university participate in a sustainability assessment?

    d. What do the results of that assessment say?

    e. Are library staff members generally supportive? If not, how can the committee work to build support?

    f. What about patrons?

    g. Is the community in general engaged with sustainability issues?

3. Relationships with outside sustainability groups

    a. What does the local sustainability community look like?

    b. What groups should the library reach out to both to support the efforts of others and to get support for changes in the library?

    c. Who are the key players in the local sustainability community?

    d. Are there regular meetings of a sustainability commission or other official group that the library should join or attend?

    e. Is there a farmers market, Transition Town group, or other local sustainability initiative the library should consider supporting with programming or collection building?

4. Sustainability programming and collections

    a. What kinds of sustainability programming does the library already do?

b. Does the library have an Earth Day program or host other kinds of programming with an environmental theme?

c. What about the collection?

d. Does it need updating or broadening?

e. For public libraries, does it include the kinds of practical information needed for families and local businesses considering things like alternative energy or teaching children about climate change?

f. For academic libraries, does it include the major theoretical works on sustainability issues as well as work on sustainability in higher education? Look at WorldCat and compare local holdings to the range of titles available on sustainability themes. Look at the bibliography provided and which titles might be valuable additions to the local collection.

5. Sustainability plan

a. Does the university or city have an existing sustainability plan?

b. How does the library fit into this plan, and how can that plan be incorporated into a library plan?

c. What is the vision for a sustainable future, and how can the library contribute to moving toward that vision?

THE ASSESSMENT TOOL—PART 2.1: ELECTRICITY

1. Measurement

a. Has your library had an energy audit or other carbon footprint assessment done?

b. Is there an institutional sustainability assessment available that might contain that information?

c. How much electricity does the library use each year, each month? Are there discernible patterns in usage, i.e., higher in the summer?

d. How is the electricity that the library uses generated?

2. Lighting

a. Determine how many different kinds lighting your library has, i.e., outside, overhead, task etc.

    b. What kinds of bulbs are currently being used and how many?

    c. Is the library currently using any solar, LED, or CFL bulbs?

    d. What about timers in the stacks or motion sensitive lights?

    e. Are all lights turned off at night?

    f. Is the security lighting adequate or excessive?

3. Heating and cooling

    a. What is the current schedule for cleaning the filter and is it actually followed?

    b. Would the building benefit from better insulation and window treatments?

    c. What temperature is the building maintained at in summer, winter? What is the library's policy on space heaters?

    d. Can this be changed to minimize energy usage while still maintaining the comfort of patrons and staff?

    e. Does the employee dress code allow appropriate seasonal clothing in the summer?

4. Computers and printers

    a. Are the computers and printers turned off every night?

    b. Are they set up to default to an energy saving mode when not in use?

    c. Has the library chosen Energy Star Rated machines?

THE ASSESSMENT TOOL—PART 2.2:
TRANSPORTATION AND THE LIBRARY

1. Employees

    a. How do most employees get to work?

    b. If employees aren't using public transport, why not?

    c. Are many employees carpooling and if not, why?

    d. What are the local public transportation choices?

    e. Does the library offer any incentives to encourage public transportation or carpooling?

    f. What about biking employees? Are there easily accessible bike racks? Is there a shower or other facility for employees to use if they need to refresh after biking to work?

g. Does the library have a telecommuting policy and is it used?

h. When employees travel out of town for conferences and other events are they encouraged to use trains instead of airplanes or cars?

2. Patrons

a. How do most patrons get to the library? Consider a survey (an in-building one) to get this information if it isn't already apparent.

b. Is the library well situated from public transport stops and if not, is this a fixable barrier?

c. Are schedules and other information about public transportation options readily available at the library?

d. Is there an existing relationship between the library and the transportation agency that can be built on for cross promotion?

e. Are programs and other events timed to make it easy for patrons to use public transportation?

f. Is the library accessible to walkers and bicyclists?

g. Are there easy landscaping or parking lot changes that can be made?

h. What else could the library do to make itself less car friendly and more friendly to alternative transportation choices?

3. Library owned vehicles

a. How many vehicles does the library own, and for what purpose are they used?

b. Are they scheduled to be replaced soon, or are they likely to be in use for the foreseeable future?

c. Are they all gasoline, or does the library own a hybrid or other alternative fuel vehicle?

d. Is there any support for purchasing a new hybrid or alternative fuel vehicle at this time?

e. Consider the existing uses of the vehicles. Can the miles driven be reduced by combining trips or replacing some with other transportation alternatives?

f. What about couriers used by local and regional consortiums?

THE ASSESSMENT TOOL—PART 3: OTHER GREEN PRACTICES

1. Solid waste

   a. Does your library have an effective recycling program in place for paper, plastic, and metals?

   b. Are bins available, accessible, and actually used by both patrons and staff?

   c. What about food waste and compostables? Is a library compost pile a workable idea? If not, is there a gardener on staff or a community garden that would welcome the library's compostable waste?

   d. What about batteries and printer cartridges? Does the library offer both staff and the public disposal bins for these?

   e. For most libraries, withdrawn books are a very large percentage of the waste stream. Consider your current procedures for these materials. Are you selling what you can and donating where possible? Do you have a contract with a book recycler for these items?

2. E-Waste

   a. How does your library currently dispose of e-waste, i.e. old computers, printers, and miscellaneous electronics?

   b. Are materials currently being properly reused or recycled? If not, check with your local waste materials handler or office of sustainability to see what options exist in your area and how your library can begin recycling these items.

3. Water usage

   a. How much water does your library use and what does it use it for? Water bills and your local water company's website should provide this information.

   b. Are green areas appropriately landscaped for your climate?

   c. Do any of the taps drip or toilets run?

   d. Are low flow toilets and automated faucets a possibility?

   e. Are there other water hungry activities specific to your library and, if so, is the water being used carefully?

4. Buying green

   a. Has your library made the switch to using post-consumer content recycled paper?

   b. Are your cleaning supplies free of hazardous chemicals, including phosphates and petrochemical-free?

   c. What about your shipping supplies, especially for interlibrary loan?

   d. Is the library choosing recycled products and reusing where possible?

THE ASSESSMENT TOOL—PART 4: LIBRARY BUDGETS

1. Diversifying funding sources

   a. Consider your library's budget and what percentage of incoming funds come from what sources. How many different sources are represented?

   b. Does your library seek out grants and support staff seeking training opportunities for grant writing?

   c. For academic libraries, does your library have a relationship with the Development Office and work to keep the library on their agenda?

   d. What kind of marketing toward donors does the library do? Would a regular newsletter or a brochure detailing how to give to the library be a useful tool?

   e. What about the Friends of the Library group? Is there one and do they have a record of successful fundraising?

   f. Are there other options for additional funding that should be pursued?

2. Considering the collection

   a. Examine your collection spending in detail, especially journal and other periodical expenses.

   b. Does the way you are spending your collection budget meet your library's particular goals?

   c. How much of your budget is tied up in large packages, ones where only a small group of the subscribed titles are getting use?

    d. What percentage of your budget is tied up in multiyear contracts and how closely is usage scrutinized before contracts are negotiated when they expire?

    e. Are you using and promoting your state-funded suite of databases?

    f. Are there other areas of the collection where spending should be directed to better meet the needs of the library's patrons?

THE ASSESSMENT TOOL—PART 5: TRANSFORMING THE INFORMATION ECOSYSTEM FROM WITHIN

1. Open access

    a. What can the library do to make an open access initiative on your campus a viable idea?

    b. Is there a conversation happening now that the library can contribute to or should the library start that conversation?

    c. Is there funding available to bring in speakers or host a symposium on open access?

    d. What about an institutional repository?

    e. How could that fit into the existing set of supports the library and institution currently offer?

    f. How could it be funded and maintained?

2. Wise licensing

    a. Review your existing licenses for objectionable terms such as not allowing interlibrary loan, limiting access for in-building users, attempts to limit the use of the resource for electronic reserves, attempts to preempt fair use doctrine, and other overreaches.

    b. Consider how these licenses can be renegotiated when they are up for renewal.

    c. Look at how much support for staff development is available to support those engaged in negotiations and consider whether it should be increased.

3. Strengthening consortiums and other interlibrary relationships

    a. Review the library's existing consortial relationships and consider what those relationships bring to library. Is the consortium working well or should the library invest time and effort in improving their consortial relationships?

b. Are there other consortia active locally that would be a good fit? What about interlibrary loan agreements?

c. Is the library active in reciprocal relationships that would reduce borrowing cost and time while at the same time contributing to the strength of the interlibrary loan system?

THE ASSESSMENT TOOL—PART 6: SUPPORTING YOUR LOCAL ECONOMY

1. Participating in the local economy

a. Consider the nonmaterials purchases your library makes. Who are your primary vendors and are there local alternatives that could competitively supply some part of your regular purchases?

b. Review your vendor lists and compare them with the locally owned businesses in your community.

c. Review your web presence and the services you currently offer to local entrepreneurs.

d. Is the collection supporting this group of patrons and are there improvements that could be made to enhance this part of the collection?

e. What about programming? Are there targeted programs for this group, perhaps workshops on finding industry and company information or one on navigating local and state regulatory information?

THE ASSESSMENT TOOL—PART 7.1: MEETING THE NEEDS OF THE LOCAL COMMUNITY

1. Serving marginalized community members

a. Which marginalized groups within your community does the library currently seek to serve through collections and programming?

b. Review the census data for your community or the demographics for your university and use it when considering the questions below.

c. Are there specific racial and ethnic groups who are represented in the community, but not in your collections or programming?

d. Does the collection reflect the linguistic makeup of the community, offering at least something for each group to read in their native language?

e. What about economic groups? Is the library making an effort to meet the needs of working class and poor patrons in proportion to their representation in the community?

f. Is there programming aimed at the interests and concerns of working class and poor members of the community?

g. Review the literacy rate of the local community using either the National Assessment of Adult Literacy or other dataset and consider whether the library should be more active in supporting and developing adult literacy programs.

h. Look at the library's existing advisory groups. Is the membership diverse or should there be a special recruitment effort to build diversity.

i. Are there local or campus based groups that the library should join to learn how to better support minority and poor patrons and to offer that support to those already involved in targeted programming?

2. The library as an employer

a. Consider the library as whole and, if possible, review the pay scales. Are they reasonable and do they meet the living wage requirements of your area? Does the library pay those lowest on the scale enough to actually live in the area? Is the difference between the highest paid employee and the lowest paid employee greater than 20?

b. Does the library create part-time jobs to avoid paying benefits or because the job makes the most sense as a part-time position?

c. What about the library's leave policies? Are they equitable and reasonable? Consider family and sick leave carefully. Would the library benefit from a more generous policy, one that allows sick employees to stay out of the workplace or care for ill family members?

d. Consider workplace democracy. Is there a forum for all library employees to have their voices heard? Is the relationship between the library administration and the union, if there is one, good? If not, what could be done to improve it?

THE ASSESSMENT TOOL—PART 7.2: PROTECTING THE RIGHT TO READ

1. Protecting fair use

   a. Is your staff well trained and do they understand both the statutory and case law surrounding fair use?

   b. Are they able to communicate that information effectively to patrons when needed?

   c. For academic libraries, how do the policies governing your reserve desk and electronic reserves align with the current best practices as laid out in the Code of Best Practices for Fair Use in Academic and Research Libraries?

   d. Are your policies reasonably risk tolerant?

   e. What about your license agreements? Are you involved in licenses that severely restrict your patrons' fair use rights and, if so, can they be renegotiated?

2. Evolving the right of first sale for the digital environment

   a. Are library staff well educated about the legal complexities involved in the lending of e-books?

   b. Are they familiar with the various alternate models and do they have the tools and the time to follow news and legal cases as they evolve?

   c. Has the library articulated a set of goals for what it wants in an e-book package and presented these goals to publishers as part of the negotiation process?

3. Guarding patron privacy

   a. Look at your library's privacy and confidentiality policies and consider whether your license agreements with vendors, including any hosted software systems, comply with that policy.

   b. If you have hosted or cloud based systems, is everyone who needs to be familiar with how they handle subpoenas and warrants?

c. Do your state laws protect privacy and if so what happens when your data is hosted in another state or even another country?

d. Consider creating a document listing your privacy priorities and the language in vendor contracts that supports or fails to support those priorities. Use that as a starting point when renegotiating contracts and when choosing new vendors.

Sample Sustainability Plan

Sustainability Vision

University library seeks to support the mission of the university and the library by becoming a sustainability leader on the campus and within the library community. University library will accomplish this by focusing our efforts on enhancing the environmental literacy of the campus and community through programming and collections, developing new green practices for our daily work, enhancing the scholarly communication system through the development of an institutional repository while encouraging and supporting open access initiatives, and putting into practice our commitment to equality and democracy by building a diverse, equitably compensated, and empowered staff.

Sustainability Committee

The sustainability committee reports to the director. Members serve two-year staggered terms, except for the assistant director who shall serve permanently ex officio. The committee will include one member from each department of the library, including reference, access services, archives, collection development, technical services, and each of the branches. Department heads will select a member of their staff, or themselves, to serve. No member may serve consecutive terms.

Outreach

Goal: University library will seek to make connections across campus with other groups working on sustainability issues.

> **Objective:** University library will gain representation on the university sustainability committee.
>
> *Action Item:* Contact campus sustainability coordinator to discuss the role of the library on campus and how we can contribute to the sustainability committee's work.
>
> *Action Item:* Read through minutes of university sustainability committee to become familiar with their work and what their goals are for the future.

> **Objective:** University library will support student groups working on sustainability issues.
>
> *Action Item:* Contact Student Life for a list of student groups and review which ones we should reach out to and offer programming or collection support.

Library Greening

Goal: University library will reduce its carbon footprint.

> **Objective:** University library will schedule an energy audit with Physical Plant and will then examine the results and add objectives as needed.
>
> *Action Item:* Schedule audit by Jan. 12.

> **Objective:** University library will encourage staff and patrons to use alternative transportation to get to the library.
>
> *Action Item:* Contact University Office of Sustainability to inquire about existing incentive programs for staff.
>
> *Action Item:* Gather relevant bus/train schedules and make them available.
>
> *Action Item:* Communicate with department heads and other managers to suggest that they work with staff to ensure that schedules are compatible with public transport.

Action Item: Develop a list of volunteers who are willing to assist if someone needs emergency transport during the day, for example, because a child is sick.

Action Item: Contact Physical Plant and ask that existing bike rack be moved to a more convenient location and repainted.

Information Economy

Goal: University library will work to build a stronger information system by supporting open access publishing on campus and off.

Objective: Create an institutional repository.

Action Item: Assemble a white paper including background information about institutional repositories, rationales for why University library should host one, and an initial budget projection.

Objective: Improve access to and visibility of open access journals in OpenURL Link Resolver.

Action Item: Contact system librarian and review which collections are turned on and off and gather a list of possible open access targets to present to reference department for review.

Equity

Goal: Improve staff development opportunities for staff at all levels.

Objective: Build a lunchtime journal club open to all staff.

Action Item: Write a proposal to present to department heads and the director including a list of publications that could be used and the history of library staff journal clubs.

Goal: Enhance staff knowledge and understanding about issues of fair use.

Objective: Offer library-funded workshop attendance at a fair use training workshop such as that at the University of Maryland or other institution.

Action Item: Consult director and ask for funding and likely candidate.

Objective: Provide opportunities for staff to attend free of charge webinars and local training events on fair use.

Action Item: Research opportunities and begin creating a list to share with staff.

Resources for Starting a Sustainability Discussion in Your Library

Sustainability Focus

Brown, Lester R. 2008. *Plan B 3.0: mobilizing to save civilization*. New York: W. W. Norton.

Dresner, Simon. *The principles of sustainability*. Sterling, VA: Earthscan Publications, 2002.

Hawken, Paul. 2007. *Blessed unrest: how the largest movement in the world came into being, and why no one saw it coming*. New York: Viking.

McKibben, Bill. 1989. *The end of nature*. New York: Random House.

Speth, James Gustave. 2008. *The bridge at the end of the world: capitalism, the environment, and crossing from crisis to sustainability*. New Haven, CT: Yale University Press.

Greening Libraries Focus

Antonelli, Monika, and Mark McCullough. 2012. *Greening libraries*. Los Angeles, CA: Library Juice Press.

Miller, Kathryn. 2010. *Public libraries going green.* Chicago: American Library Association.

Mulford, Sam McBane, and Ned A. Himmel. 2010. *How green is my library?* Santa Barbara, CA: Libraries Unlimited.

Library Values Focus

American Library Association. 2002. *Intellectual freedom manual.* Chicago: American Library Association.

Gorman, Michael. 2000. *Our enduring values: librarianship in the 21st century.* Chicago: American Library Association.

Shera, Jesse Hauk. 1969. *The silent stir of thought: or, what the computer cannot do.* Geneseo, NY: The College.

Services to Marginalized Patrons Focus

Big 12 Plus Libraries Consortium Diversity Conference, Teresa Y. Neely, and Kuang-Hwei Lee-Smeltzer. 2002. *Diversity now: people, collections, and services in academic libraries: selected papers from the Big 12 Plus Libraries Consortium Diversity Conference.* New York: Haworth Information Press.

Osborne, Robin. 2004. From *outreach to equity: innovative models of library policy and practice.* Chicago: American Library Association.

Smallwood, Carol, and Kim Becnel. 2013. *Library services for multicultural patrons: strategies to encourage library use.* Metuchen, NJ: Scarecrow Press.

Bibliography

Association for the Advancement of Sustainability in Higher Education. *Stars Technical Manual*. October 2013. www.aashe.org/files/documents/STARS/2.0/stars_2.0.1_technical_manual.pdf.

Alliance for Taxpayer Access. "National Institutes of Health Public Access Policy." Accessed December 12, 2013. www.taxpayeraccess.org/issues/nih/index.shtml.

Alliance for Taxpayer Access. "Who Opposes the Fair Copyright in Research Works Act." Accessed December 13, 2013. www.taxpayeraccess.org/issues/opposition/index.shtml.

Adams, John D. "Six Dimensions of Mental Models." In *The Sustainable Enterprise Fieldbook: When It All Comes Together*, edited by Jeana Wirtenberg, William G. Russell, and David Lipsky. New York: AMACOM Books, 2009. 60–69.

Adler, Prudence S., Patricia Aufderheide, Brandon Butler, and Peter Jaszi. *Code of Best Practices in Fair Use for Academic and Research Libraries*. Washington, DC: Association of Research Libraries, 2012.

Agardy, Tundi, Neville J. Ash, H. David Cooper, Sandra Díaz, Daniel P. Faith, Georgina Mace, Jeffrey A. McNeely, et al. *Ecosystems and Human Well-Being: Biodiversity Synthesis*. Washington, DC: World Resources Institute, 2005.

Agyeman, Julian, Robert D. Bullard, and Bob Evans. "Exploring the Nexus: Bringing Together Sustainability, Environmental Justice and Equity." *Space & Polity* 6, no. 1 (April 1, 2002): 77–90.

Albanese, Andrew Richard. "A Failure to Communicate." *Publishers Weekly*. June 4, 2010. www.publishersweekly.com/pw/by-topic/industry-news/publisher-news/article/43500-a-failure-to-communicate.html.

American College & University Presidents' Climate Commitment. www.presidents climatecommitment.org.

American Library Association. "James Madison Award." Accessed December 13, 2013. www.ala.org/awardsgrants/james-madison-award.

American Public Health Association. "Addressing the Urgent Threat of Global Climate Change to Public Health and the Environment." November 6, 2007. www.apha .org/advocacy/policy/policysearch/default.htm?id=1351.

Anderson, Kevin, and Alice Bows. "Beyond 'Dangerous' Climate Change: Emission Scenarios for a New World." *Philosophical Transactions of the Royal Society A: Mathematical, Physical and Engineering Sciences* 369, no. 1934 (January 13, 2011): 20–44.

Antonelli, Monika. "The Green Library Movement: An Overview and Beyond." *Electronic Green Journal*, no. 27 (Fall 2008): 1–11.

Arnold, Douglas N., and Henry Cohn. "Mathematicians Take a Stand." *Notices of the AMS* 59, no. 6 (2012): 828–33.

Art Daily. "New York Public Library Faces Harshest Budget Cut in Its History." May 8, 2010. http://artdaily.com/news/37928/New-York-Public-Library-Faces -Harshest-Budget-Cut-In-Its-History#.UoUHSiRQ2Ho.

Bade, David W. *Responsible Librarianship: Library Policies for Unreliable Systems*. Duluth, MN: Library Juice Press, 2007.

Bahro, Rudolf. *From Red to Green: Interviews with New Left Review*. London: Verso, 1984.

Barboza, David, and Keith Bradsher. "In China, a Labor Movement Aided by Modern Technology." *New York Times*, June 16, 2010.

Barnett, T. P., and D. W. Pierce. "Sustainable Water Deliveries from the Colorado River in a Changing Climate." *Proceedings of the National Academy of Sciences of the United States of America* 106, no. 18 (2009): 7334–38. www.ncbi.nlm.nih.gov/pubmed/19380718.

Barnosky, Anthony D. "Has the Earth's Sixth Mass Extinction Already Arrived?" *Nature* 471, no. 7336 (2011): 51–57.

Bartolino, J. R., and W. L. Cunningham. "Ground-Water Depletion across the Nation." Reston, VA: US Geological Survey, 2003.

Beghtol, Clare. "Professional Values and Ethics in Knowledge Organization and Cataloging." *Journal of Information Ethics* 17, no. 1 (March 1, 2008): 12–19.

Bloomberg News. "iPhone Workers Say 'Meaningless' Life Sparks Suicides." June 2, 2010. www.bloomberg.com/news/2010-06-02/foxconn-workers-in-china-say-meaningless-life-monotony-spark-suicides.html.

"Books, Magazines, and Newspaper Industries." Center for Responsive Politics. www.opensecrets.org. accessed April 26, 2014.

Bort, Julie. "The American Library Association Has Given Aaron Swartz Its First Ever Posthumous Award." *Business Insider* (2013).

Bourg, Chris. "My Short Stint on the JLA Editorial Board." *Feral Librarian* (blog) (March 23, 2013). http://chrisbourg.wordpress.com/2013/03/23/my-short-stint-on-the-jla-editorial-board.

———. "My Short Stint on the JLA Editorial Board." *Feral Librarian* (blog) (March 29, 2013). http://chrisbourg.wordpress.com/2013/03/29/my-stint-on-the-jla-editorial-board-a-few-clarifications.

Boyle, James. "The Second Enclosure Movement and the Construction of the Public Domain." *Law and Contemporary Problems* 66, no. 1/2 (2003): 33–74.

Brown, Donald A. *Climate Change Ethics: Navigating the Perfect Moral Storm*. Abingdon, UK: Routledge, 2013.

Brown, Laura. "JSTOR—Free Access to Early Journal Content and Serving 'Unaffiliated' Users." JSTOR, news release, September 7, 2011. http://about.jstor.org/news/jstor%E2%80%93free-access-early-journal-content-and-serving-%E2%80%9Cunaffiliated%E2%80%9D-users.

Brown, Lester R. *The Twenty-Ninth Day: Accommodating Human Needs and Numbers to the Earth's Resources*. New York: Norton, 1978.

———. *World on the Edge: How to Prevent Environmental and Economic Collapse*. New York: W. W. Norton, 2011.

Budd, John M. "Toward a Practical and Normative Ethics for Librarianship." *Library Quarterly* 76, no. 3 (2006): 251–69.

Bundy, Mary Lee, and Frederick J. Stielow. *Activism in American Librarianship, 1962–1973*. New York: Greenwood Press, 1987.

Buschmann, John. *Dismantling the Public Sphere: Situating and Sustaining Librarianship in the Age of the New Public Philosophy*. Westport, CN: Libraries Unlimited, 2003.

Calhoun, Karen. *The Changing Nature of the Catalog and Its Integration with Other Discovery Tools. Special report prepared at the request of the Library of Congress* (March 17, 2006).

Carlson, Scott. "Frustration with Green Rankings Pushes Colleges to Develop Their Own." *Chronicle of Higher Education* 56, no. 31 (2010): A16.

Center for Responsive Politics. "American Library Assn." Influence & Lobbying. Accessed December 12, 2013. www.opensecrets.org/lobby/clientsum.php?id=D000046971&year=2012.

Clark, David. "Mathematical Publishing, Part III: Elsevier's Response to 'the Cost of Knowledge.'" London Mathematical Society newsletter, no. 412 (March 2012). http://old.lms.ac.uk/newsletter/412/412_issue.pdf.

Climate Group. *SMART 2020: Enabling the Low Carbon Economy in the Information Age.* Creative Commons, 2008. www.smart2020.org/_assets/files/02_Smart 2020Report.pdf.

Coristine, Laura E., and Jeremy T. Kerr. "Habitat Loss, Climate Change, and Emerging Conservation Challenges in Canada." *Canadian Journal of Zoology* 89, no. 5 (2011): 435–51.

Costanza, Robert, Ralph d'Arge, Rudolf de Groot, Stephen Farber, Monica Grasso, Bruce Hannon, Karin Limburg, et al. "The Value of the World's Ecosystem Services and Natural Capital." *Nature* 387, no. 6630 (1997): 253–60.

Costello, Jean. "Library Bypass Strategies." The Radical Patron: Extreme Thoughts on Public Libraries, www.radicalpatron.com/library-bypass-strategies.

Daly, Herman E. *Ecological Economics and Sustainable Development: Selected Essays of Herman Daly.* Cheltenham, UK: Edward Elgar, 2007.

Daly, Herman E. *Steady-State Economics.* 2nd Ed. Washington, DC: Island Press, 1991.

Daly, Herman E., and Joshua C. Farley. *Ecological Economics: Principles and Applications.* Washington: Island Press, 2004.

Danner, Richard A., and Barbara Bintliff. "Academic Freedom Issues for Academic Librarians." *Legal Reference Services Quarterly* 25, no. 4 (2006): 13–35.

Davis, Philip M. "Where to Spend Our E-journal Money? Defining a University Library's Core Collection Through Citation Analysis." *Portal: Libraries & the Academy* 2, no. 1 (January 2002): 155–66.

de Jong, Mark. "Good Negotiations: Strategies for Negotiating Vendor Contracts." *Bottom Line: Managing Library Finances* 22, no. 2 (2009): 37–41.

De Rosa, Cathy, Lorcan Dempsey, and Alane Wilson et al. The OCLC 2003 Environmental Scan: Pattern Recognition. Dublin, OH: OCLC, 2003.

Devuyst, Dimitri. "Linking Impact Assessment and Sustainable Development at the Local Level: The Introduction of Sustainability Assessment Systems." *Sustainable Development* 8, no. 2 (2000): 67–78.

Dresner, Simon. *The Principles of Sustainability.* Sterling, VA: Earthscan Publications, 2002.

Dupuis, John. "Library Vendors, Politics, Aaron Swartz, #pdftribute." *Confessions of a Science Librarian, ScienceBlogs.* http://scienceblogs.com/confessions/2013/01/17/library-vendors-politics-aaron-swartz-pdftribute.

Durley, Rev. Dr. Gerald. "Why Climate Change Is a Civil Rights Issue." HuffPost, Black Voices, www.huffingtonpost.com/rev-dr-gerald-durley/climate-change-civil-rights_b_3844986.html?.

Ecosystems and Human Well-Being: Biodiversity Synthesis. World Resources Institute, 2005.

England, Andrew. "Saudis to Phase out Wheat Production by 2016." *Financial Times,* April 11, 2008, 9.

Environment News Service. "Climate Change Blamed for Thai Floods as UN Climate Talks Open." April 6, 2011. www.ens-newswire.com/ens/apr2011/2011-04-06 -02.html.

Ephraim, Philip E. "The Greening of Libraries." *Library Management* 24, no. 3 (2003): 160–63.

Esposito, Joseph J. "Open Access 2.0: Access to Scholarly Publications Moves to a New Phase." *Journal of Electronic Publishing* 11, no. 2 (2008).

Estabrook, Leigh. "Productivity, Profit, and Libraries." *Library Journal* 106, no. 13 (1981): 1377.

Farrow, Scott. "Environmental Equity and Sustainability: Rejecting the Kaldor-Hicks Criteria." *Ecological Economics* 27, no. 2 (1998): 183–88.

Finneran, Michael. "Wildfires: A Symptom of Climate Change." NASA, September 24, 2010, www.nasa.gov/topics/earth/features/wildfires.html.

Fogarty, David. "Scientists See Climate Change Link to Australian Floods." *Reuters.* Published electronically January 12, 2011. www.reuters.com/article/2011/01/ 12/us-climate-australia-floods-idUSTRE70B1XF20110112.

Gard, David L., and Gregory A. Keoleian. "Digital Versus Print: Energy Performance in the Selection and Use of Scholarly Journals." *Journal of Industrial Ecology* 6, no. 2 (2003): 115–32.

Gardiner, Stephen M. *A Perfect Moral Storm: The Ethical Tragedy of Climate Change.* New York: Oxford University Press, 2013.

"Global Warming Puts the Arctic on Thin Ice." Natural Resources Defense Council, November 22, 2005, www.nrdc.org/globalwarming/qthinice.asp.

Gorman, Michael. *Our Enduring Values: Librarianship in the 21st Century.* Chicago: American Library Association, 2000.

Gowers, Timothy. "Elsevier—My Part in Its Downfall." *Gowers's Weblog: Mathematics Relatated Discussions.* http://gowers.wordpress.com/2012/01/21/elsevier-my -part-in-its-downfall.

Grant, Carl. "Another Facet of the 'Library Bypass Strategies,'" *Thoughts from Carl Grant* (blog), November 16, 2009. http://thoughts.care-affiliates.com/2009/11/ another-facet-of-library-bypass.html.

Gronewold, Nathaniel. "Is the Flooding in Pakistan a Climate Change Disaster?" Climatewire, Scientific American, August 18, 2010, www.scientificamerican.com/ article.cfm?id=is-the-flooding-in-pakist.

Grynbaum, Michael M. "24-Hour Read-in Protests Cuts to Libraries." *New York Times*, June 13, 2010. www.nytimes.com/2010/06/14/nyregion/14shush .html?_r=0.

Guédon, Jean-Claude. "The Digital Library: An Oxymoron?" *Bulletin of the Medical Library Association* 87 (1999): 9–19.

———. *In Oldenburg's Long Shadow: Librarians, Research Scientists, Publishers, and the Control of Scientific Publishing.* Washington, DC: Association of Research Libraries, 2001.

Hall, Charles A. S., and John W. Day Jr. "Revisiting the Limits to Growth after Peak Oil." *American Scientist* 97, no. 3 (2009): 230–37.

Hansen, James, Makiko Sato, Pushker Kharecha, David Beerling, Robert Berner, Valerie Masson-Delmotte, Mark Pagani, et al. "Target Atmospheric CO_2: Where Should Humanity Aim?" *Open Atmospheric Science Journal* 2, no. 1 (2008): 217–31.

Hardin, Garrett. "The Tragedy of the Commons." *Science* 162, no. 3859 (December 13, 1968): 1243–48.

Harris, Michael H., and Stan A. Hannah. *Into the Future: The Foundations of Library and Information Services in the Post-Industrial Era.* Norwood, NJ: Ablex, 1993.

Harris, Paul G. *World Ethics and Climate Change: From International to Global Justice.* Edinburgh University Press, 2010.

Harris, Roma M. *Librarianship: The Erosion of a Woman's Profession.* Norwood, NJ: Ablex, 1992.

Hassinik, Laura, and David Clark. "Elsevier's Response to the Mathematics Community." *Notices of the AMS* 59, no. 6 (2012): 833–35.

Hawken, Paul. *Blessed Unrest: How the Largest Movement in the World Came into Being, and Why No One Saw It Coming.* New York: Viking, 2007. http://catdir.loc.gov/ catdir/toc/ecip076/2006101145.html.

Hawkinson, John A. "Swartz Indicted for Breaking and Entering." *The Tech* (MIT newspaper), November 18, 2011.

Hayden, Maureen. "Opponents of Amendment to Put Tax Caps in Constitution Face Uphill Battle." *Herald Bulletin*, October 6, 2010.

Helmer, Jodi. "Environmental Education: Going Green Is a Library-Wide Effort." *Library Media Connection* 28, no. 4 (2010): 22–23.

Hess, Charlotte, and Elinor Ostrom. "Introduction: An Overview of the Knowledge Commons." In *Understanding Knowledge as a Commons: From Theory to Practice*, edited by Charlotte Hess and Elinor Ostrom. Cambridge, MA: MIT Press, 2007.

Hoerling, Martin. "Preliminary Assessment of Climate Factors Contributing to the Extreme 2011 Tornadoes" (draft research assessment). Physical Sciences Division, Earth System Research Laboratory, National Oceanic and Atmospheric Administration. July 8, 2011.

Hoeschele, Wolfgang. *Economics of Abundance: A Political Economy of Freedom, Equity, and Sustainability*. Farnham, Surrey, GBR: Ashgate Publishing Group, 2010.

Holling, C. S. "Resilience and Stability of Ecological Systems." *Annual Review of Ecology and Systematics* 4 (1973): 1–23.

Immerzeel, Walter W., Ludovicus P. H. van Beek, and Marc F. P. Bierkens. "Climate Change Will Affect the Asian Water Towers." *Science* 328, no. 5984 (June 11, 2010): 1382–85.

International Energy Agency. "Monthly Oil Data Survey." Accessed December 13, 2013. www.iea.org/statistics/relatedsurveys/monthlyoildatasurvey.

Jacobs, Michael. "Sustainable Development as a Contested Concept." In *Fairness and Futurity: Essays on Environmental Sustainability and Social Justice*, edited by Andrew Dobson. New York: Oxford University Press, 1999.

Jastram, Iris. "Heads They Win, Tails We Lose: Discovery Tools Will Never Deliver on Their Promise." *Pegasus Librarian* (blog). http://pegasuslibrarian.com/2011/01/heads-they-win-tales-we-lose-discovery-tools-will-never-deliver-on-their-promise.html. n2.

Johnson, Greg. "Greening Our Libraries: Practical Advice for Saving the Planet and Your Budget." *Mississippi Libraries* 73, no. 4 (Winter2009): 86–88.

JSTOR. "JSTOR Statement: Misuse Incident and Criminal Case." News release, July 19, 2011. http://about.jstor.org/news/jstor-statement-misuse-incident-and-criminal-case.

Jucker, Rolf. "Have the Cake and Eat It: Ecojustice Versus Development? Is It Possible to Reconcile Social and Economic Equity, Ecological Sustainability, and Human Development? Some Implications for Ecojustice Education." *Educational Studies* 36, no. 1 (2004): 10–26.

Kaye, Jeffrey." In China, Factory Workers Allege Poisoning from iPhone Production." *PBS NewsHour* video, 7:25. April 13, 2011. www.pbs.org/newshour/bb/world/jan-june11/china_04-13.html.

Kelley, Michael. "Bloomberg Proposes Cutting NYC Library Funding by Nearly $100 Million." *Library Journal* (February 8, 2012). http://lj.libraryjournal.com/2012/02/opinion/john-berry/bloomberg-proposes-cutting-library-funding-by-nearly-100-million.

———. "In California, All State Funding for Public Libraries Remains in Jeopardy." *Library Journal* (July 5, 2011). http://lj.libraryjournal.com/2011/07/budgets-funding/in-california-all-state-funding-for-public-libraries-remains-in-jeopardy.

———. "Texas Governor Signs Budget Cutting State Funding for Library Services by 88%." *Library Journal* (July 29, 2011). http://lj.libraryjournal.com/2011/07/budgets-funding/texas-governor-signs-budget-cutting-state-funding-for-library-services-by-88-percent/#_.

Kniffel, Leonard. "Cuts, Freezes Widespread in Academic Libraries." *American Libraries* 40, no. 67 (2009): 28.

Lagi, M., Yavni Bar-Yam, K. Z. Bertrand, and Yaneer Bar-Yam. "The Food Crises: A Quantitative Model of Food Prices Including Speculators and Ethanol Conversion." New England Complex Systems Institute. Submitted September 21, 2011. http://arxiv.org/abs/1109.4859.

Lankes, R. David. *The Atlas of New Librarianship*. Cambridge, MA: MIT Press, 2011. http://mitpress-ebooks.mit.edu/product/atlas-new-librarianship.

Leiss, William. *The Domination of Nature*. New York: G. Braziller, 1972.

Lemley, Trey, Robert M. Britton, and Jie Li. "Negotiating Your License." *Journal of Electronic Resources in Medical Libraries* 8, no. 4 (2011): 325–38.

Lubin, David A., and Daniel C. Esty. "The Sustainability Imperative." *Harvard Business Review*, 88, no. 5 (2010): 42–50.

Mann, Michael E. "Defining Dangerous Anthropogenic Interference." *Proceedings of the National Academy of Sciences of the United States of America* 106, no. 11 (2009): 4065–66.

McCabe, Mark J., Christopher M. Snyder, and Anna Fagin. "Open Access Versus Traditional Journal Pricing: Using a Simple 'Platform Market' Model to Understand Which Will Win (and Which Should)." *Journal of Academic Librarianship* 39, no. 1 (2013): 11–19.

McGuigan, Glenn S. , and Robert D. Russell. "The Business of Academic Publishing: A Strategic Analysis of the Academic Journal Publishing Industry and Its Impact on the Future of Scholarly Publishing." *Electronic Journal of Academic and Special Librarianship* 9, no. 3 (2008). http://southernlibrarianship.icaap.org/content/v09n03/mcguigan_g01.html.

McKibben, Bill. *Eaarth: Making a Life on a Tough New Planet*. New York: Times Books, 2010.

———. "Global Warming's Terrifying New Math." *Rolling Stone*, no. 1162 (2012). www.rollingstone.com/politics/news/global-warmings-terrifying-new-math-20120719.

Meadows, Donella. "Envisioning a Sustainable World." October 8, 2012. www.donellameadows.org/archives/envisioning-a-sustainable-world.

Meadows, Donella H. *The Limits to Growth; a Report for the Club of Rome's Project on the Predicament of Mankind*. New York: Universe Books, 1972.

Merrett, Christopher. "The Expropriation of Intellectual Capital and the Political Economy of International Academic Publishing." *Critical Arts: A South-North Journal of Cultural & Media Studies* 20, no. 1 (2006): 96–111.

Morrison, Heather. "Freedom for Scholarship in the Internet Age." Simon Fraser University, 2012.

Mulford, Sam McBane, and Ned A. Himmel. *How Green Is My Library?* Santa Barbara, CA: Libraries Unlimited, 2010.

Nashville Weather Forecast Office. "Epic Flood Event of May 2010."Nashville, TN. Published electronically February 22, 2011. www.srh.noaa.gov/news/display _cmsstory.php?wfo=ohx&storyid=51780&source=0%3E.

National Wildlife Federation. "Tar Sands." www.nwf.org/What-We-Do/Energy-and -Climate/Drilling-and-Mining/Tar-Sands.aspx. Accessed April 26, 2014.

Natural Resources Defense Council. "Global Warming Puts the Arctic on Thin Ice." Last modified November 22, 2005. www.nrdc.org/globalwarming/qthinice.asp.

Natural Resources Defense Council. "Risky Gas Drilling." www.nrdc.org/energy/ gasdrilling. Accessed April 26, 2014.

Ness, Barry, Evelin Urbel-Piirsalu, Stefan Anderberg, and Lennart Olsson. "Categorising Tools for Sustainability Assessment." *Ecological Economics* 60, no. 3 (2007): 498–508.

New, Mark, et al. "Four degrees and beyond: the potential for a global temperature increase of four degrees and its implications." Special issue, *Philosophical Transactions of the Royal Society A* 369 no. 1934. (2011).

Neylon, Tyler. "The Cost of Knowledge." December 13, 2013. http://thecostof knowledge.com.

———. "Life after Elsevier: Making Open Access to Scientific Knowledge a Reality." *Guardian.* www.theguardian.com/science/blog/2012/apr/24/life-elsevier-open -access-scientific-knowledge.

Norgaard, Kari. *Living in Denial: Climate Change, Emotions, and Everyday Life.* Cambridge, MA: MIT Press, 2011.

Odlyzko, Andrew. "Open Access, Library and Publisher Competition, and the Evolution of General Commerce." Preprint. Submitted February 5, 2013. http:// arxiv.org/abs/1302.1105.

———. "The Rapid Evolution of Scholarly Communication." Learned Publishing 15, no. 1 (January 2002): 7–19. www.dtc.umn.edu/~odlyzko/doc/rapid.evolution.pdf.

Offensend, David G. *Report of the Treasurer.* New York City Public Library, 2009. http://annualreports.nypl.org/2009/treasurer.html.

Oreskes, Naomi, and Erik M. Conway. *Merchants of Doubt: How a Handful of Scientists Obscured the Truth on Issues from Tobacco Smoke to Global Warming.* 1st US ed. New York: Bloomsbury Press, 2010.

Ostrom, Elinor. *Governing the Commons: The Evolution of Institutions for Collective Action.* New York: Cambridge University Press, 1990.

Ott, Konrad, and Philipp Pratap Thapa, ed. *Greifswald's Environmental Ethics: From the Work of the Michael Otto Professorship at Ernst Moritz Arndt University 1997–2002.* Greifswald, Germany: Steinbecker, 2003.

Padilla, Emilio. "Intergenerational Equity and Sustainability." *Ecological Economics* 41, no. 1 (2002): 69–83.

Polanyi, Karl. *The Great Transformation: The Political and Economic Origins of Our Time.* Boston, MA: Beacon Press, 2001.

Pope-Chappell, Maya. "N.Y. Librarians Fight Budget Cuts, Pledge 'We Will Not Be Shushed.'" Metropolis. *Wall Street Journal.* http://blogs.wsj.com/metropolis/ 2010/06/14/ny-librarians-fight-budget-cuts-pledge-we-will-not-be-shushed.

Quick, Miriam, Ella Hollowood, and David McCandless. "How Many Gigatons of Carbon Dioxide? The Information Is Beautiful Guide to Doha." *DataBlog, Guardian.* www.theguardian.com/news/datablog/2012/dec/07/carbon-dioxide -doha-information-beautiful#_.

Randle, Keith. "The White-Coated Worker: Professional Autonomy in a Period of Change." *Work, Employment & Society* 10, no. 4 (1996): 737–53.

Ranganathan, S. R. *The Five Laws of Library Science.* Madras, London: Madras Library Association; E. Goldston, 1931.

Rees, William E. "Ecological Footprints and Appropriated Carrying Capacity: What Urban Economics Leaves Out." *Environment and Urbanization* 4, no. 2 (1992): 121–30.

Rogers, Michael et al. "In NYC, 22% Proposed Library Budget Cut." *Library Journal* 134, no. 10 (2009): 12.

Romm, Joe. "Exclusive Interview: NCAR's Trenberth on the Link between Global Warming and Extreme Deluges." *Climate Progress.* Accessed October 22, 2013. http://thinkprogress.org/climate/2010/06/14/206133/ncar-trenberth-global -warming-extreme-weather-rain-deluge.

Ryan, Marianne, and Julie Garrison. "What Do We Do Now? A Case for Abandoning Yesterday and Making the Future." *Reference & User Services Quarterly* 51, no. 1 (Fall 2011): 12–14.

Salt, David, and B. H. Walker. *Resilience Thinking: Sustaining Ecosystems and People in a Changing World.* Washington, DC: Island Press, 2006.

Save NYC Libraries. "Book Seeding in NYC." News release. *Liswire,* May 21, 2012. http://liswire.com/content/book-seeding-nyc.

———. "New Library Cuts for FY'12." Libraries Are New York. February 22, 2011. www.savenyclibraries.com/?p=319.

———. "Once More Unto the Breach!" Libraries Are New York. April 17, 2013. www.savenyclibraries.com/?p=1010.

———. "To the Stacks!" Libraries Are New York. February 13, 2012. www.savenyc libraries.com/?p=676.

———. "Victory." Libraries Are New York. July 9, 2013. www.savenyclibraries .com/?p=1148.

Schiller, Herbert I. *Culture, Inc.: The Corporate Takeover of Public Expression.* New York: Oxford University Press, 1989.

Science Daily. "Planes, Trains, or Automobiles: Travel Choices for a Smaller Carbon Footprint." (June 17, 2013).

Sharp, Gene. *The Politics of Nonviolent Action: Part One, Power and Struggle.* Boston: Porter Sargent, 1973.

———. *The Politics of Nonviolent Action: Part Two, The Methods of Nonviolent Action.* Boston: Porter Sargent, 1973.

Shera, Jesse Hauk. *"The Compleat Librarian" and Other Essays.* Cleveland, OH: Press of Case Western University, 1971.

———. "Librarians against Machines. Librarians Are Having Difficulty Adopting the New Technology Because They Have No Professional Philosophy." *Science* 156, no. 3776 (1967): 746.

———. *The Silent Stir of Thought: Or, What the Computer Cannot Do.* Geneseo, NY: The College, 1969.

———. *Sociological Foundations of Librarianship.* New York: Asia Pub. House, 1970.

———. *Toward a Theory of Librarianship: Papers in Honor of Jesse Hauk Shera.* Metuchen, NJ: Scarecrow Press, 1973.

Shiva, Vandana. *Earth Democracy: Justice, Sustainability, and Peace.* Cambridge, MA: South End Press, 2005.

Shorter, Gary. *The "Pay Ratio Provision" in the Dodd-Frank Act: Legislation to Repeal It in the 113th Congress.* Washington, DC: Library of Congress, Congressional Research Service, October 28, 2013.

Simon, Julian Lincoln. *The Ultimate Resource.* Princeton, NJ: Princeton University Press, 1981.

Smith, Joel B. "Assessing Dangerous Climate Change through an Update of the Intergovernmental Panel on Climate Change (IPCC) 'Reasons for Concern.'" *Proceedings of the National Academy of Sciences of the United States of America* 106, no. 11, (2008): 4133–37.

Sokolov, A. P., P. H. Stone, C. E. Forest, R. Prinn, M. C. Sarofim, M. Webster, S. Paltsev, et al. "Probabilistic Forecast for Twenty-First-Century Climate Based on Uncertainties in Emissions (without Policy) and Climate Parameters." *Journal of Climate* 22, no. 19 (2009): 5175–204.

Spanne, Autumn. "Colombia's Cities Risk Deluge from Changes in Andes Climate." *The Daily Climate.* December 3, 2012. www.dailyclimate.org/tdc-newsroom/2012/12/colombia-andes-flooding.

Speth, James Gustave. *The Bridge at the End of the World: Capitalism, the Environment, and Crossing from Crisis to Sustainability.* New Haven, CT: Yale University Press, 2008.

Stephens, E. "Professional Status of Librarianship Revisited." July 12, 1986.

Swartz, Aaron. "Guerilla Open Access Manifesto." http://ia600808.us.archive.org/17/items/GuerillaOpenAccessManifesto/Goamjuly2008.pdf.

Turner, Graham. "A Comparison of the Limits to Growth with Thirty Years of Reality." CSIRO Working Paper 2008-09, Socio-Economics and the Environment in Discussion, Commonwealth Scientific and Industrial Research Organisation, Australia, June 2008.

UC Berkeley Libraries. "Hot Topics: Publisher Mergers." November 8, 2011. www.lib .berkeley.edu/scholarlycommunication/publisher_mergers.html.

United Nations, World Commission on Environment and Development. "Our Common Future." 1987.

US Department of Commerce, NOAA, Earth System Research Laboratory. "Trends in Carbon Dioxide." May 6, 2013. www.esrl.noaa.gov/gmd/ccgg/trends.

US Department of Commerce, NOAA, National Weather Service. "May 2010 Epic Flood Event" (In En-US). October 17, 2010.

US Energy Information Administration. *Annual Energy Review*. Washington, DC: GPO, November 25, 2013.

——. *Emissions of Greenhouse Gases in the United States 2009*. Washington, DC, March 2011.

——. "Monthly Energy Review." Washington, DC: GPO, November 2013.

——. "Total Crude Oil and Petroleum Products." 2012. www.eia.gov/dnav/pet/ pet_cons_psup_dc_nus_mbblpd_a.htm.

Vaidhyanathan, Siva. *The Anarchist in the Library: How the Clash between Freedom and Control Is Hacking the Real World and Crashing the System*. New York: Basic Books, 2004.

Webster, Frank, and Kevin Robins. *Information Technology: A Luddite Analysis*. Norwood, NJ: Ablex, 1986.

Wilson, Pauline. *Stereotype and Status: Librarians in the United States*. Contributions in Librarianship and Information Science, no. 41. Westport, CN: Greenwood Press, 1982.

Wilson, Tony. "Sentiment and Sustainability in the Modern Library." *Alki* 27, no. 1 (March 2011): 14–16.

Wright, Curtis H. *Jesse Shera, Librarianship and Information Science*. Provo, UT: School of Library and Information Sciences, Brigham Young University, 1988.

Yohe, Gary, and Emily van Engel. "Equity and Sustainability over the Next Fifty Years: An Exercise in Economic Visioning." *Environment, Development and Sustainability* 6, no. 4 (2005): 393–413.

Index